Syntax and Style

in Old English

medieval & renaissance texts & studies

VOLUME 5

Syntax and Style in Old English

A Comparison of the Two Versions of Wærferth's Translation of Gregory's Dialogues

BY

David Yerkes

medieval & renaissance texts & studies
Center for Medieval & Early Renaissance Studies
Binghamton, New York
1982

Center for Medieval and Early Renaissance Studies
State University of New York at Binghamton
Binghamton, New York

Library of Congress Cataloging in Publication Data

Yerkes, David, 1950–
    Syntax and style in Old English.

    (Medieval & Renaissance texts & studies; 5)
    Bibliography.
    1. Gregory I, Pope, ca. 540–604. Dialogi
de vita. 2. Gregory I, Pope, ca. 540–604—
Translations, Anglo-Saxon. 3. Wærferth, Bp. of
Worcester, d. 915. 4. Anglo-Saxon language—
Syntax. 5. Anglo-Saxon language—Style.
I. Title. II. Series.
PR1552.W33Y39   270.2'092'2   81–14200
ISBN 0-86698-011-3   AACR2

Printed in the United States of America

To Bruce Mitchell

Contents

Introduction 9
Chapter 1: The Use of Parts of Speech 13
Chapter 2: Repetitions of Phrase or Clause Elements . . 39
Chapter 3: Word Order within Phrases or Clauses 48
Chapter 4: The Use of Phrases and Clauses 65
Conclusion 82
Notes 85
Bibliography 103

Introduction

OLD ENGLISH SCRIBES routinely respelled their exemplars, occasionally substituted one word for another, but seldom recast syntax. Collating the manuscripts of a typical prose text yields innumerable spelling differences, some differences in vocabulary, few if any important syntactical changes.[1] The translation of Gregory's *Dialogues*, however, constitutes an outstanding exception, for an anonymous Reviser altered the vocabulary and syntax of the original translation as systematically as he altered its spelling. The translation thus offers a perhaps unique chance to see developments in the Old English language, or at least many of the stylistic choices available to its writers. I have dealt elsewhere with the differences of vocabulary between the two versions of the *Dialogues*;[2] the present work examines their syntactical differences.

Bishop Wærferth of Worcester translated the *Dialogues* into English at King Alfred's command sometime between the early 870s and early 890s, and the revising of the translation took place roughly a century or century and a half later between 950 and 1050, probably at Worcester.[3] Wærferth presided at Worcester but may have come from another part of the country. Whether the Reviser worked at Worcester or not, his vocabulary agrees remarkably with that of Æthelwold, a native of Winchester and bishop there from 963 until his death in 984.[4] The Reviser consulted the Latin throughout, and indeed many of his changes bring the wording of the translation closer to that of Gregory. Many other changes, however, take the wording further away, and still others allow the translation about its original measure of resemblance to Gregory's Latin. Owing nothing to the Latin, instances of the last two kinds of alteration presumably bear witness to the Reviser's own idiom: to his dialect of Old English, separated in time and perhaps place from that of Wærferth, or to his stylistic preferences. The same may also hold for some alterations of the first kind, if the wording desired by the Reviser just happened to have agreed with that which he found in the Latin.

Many of the Reviser's changes make the translation more modern, bring the syntax into closer accord with that of present-day English; others have no effect on its modernity. Occasionally, though, a change leaves the translation less modern. For instance, uninfluenced by the Latin the Reviser often replaced Wærferth's prepositions with postpositions or verbal prefixes. Perhaps the Reviser simply adopted a different style from that Wærferth had chosen, and their dialects did not diverge over the treatment of prepositions and postpositions. If the dialects did differ, perhaps the Reviser's lay outside the mainstream, Wærferth's inside, and the trend toward postpositions prevailed only in dialects that contributed little to the ultimate development of English. A third explanation: English doubled back upon itself. A tenth- or eleventh-century movement away from prepositions subsequently retreated; influences came into play that by chance led English back to where it had stood in the ninth century.[5] Which linguistic features show Wærferth's or the Reviser's style, which the nonliterary norms of their language? Only comparison of their writings with all other surviving Old English texts can answer the question.[6]

Though separated by no more that 175 years and possibly by as little as 60 or 70, the revision and the original translation differ to a far greater extent than do our prose and that of, say, Emerson or Arnold. The Reviser modified Wærferth's prose the way one might Ascham's. This too may mean that the Old

English writers represent different dialects: literacy, whose spread began in earnest after the invention of printing and accelerated during the nineteenth and twentieth centuries, has so obscured the once sharp distinctions among dialects that today "the very conception of 'a variety of English' is waning in value."[7] But what if Wærferth and the Reviser both came from Worcester, which they well may have? Then either English syntax — at least as manifested in writing — used to change more rapidly than it does today, or the Reviser thought that Wærferth's style needed a lot of improving, or both. Printing froze spelling; we spell essentially the way Caxton did and almost exactly in the manner of some Elizabethan printers. Syntax, or writing style, has changed since Caxton's time, but perhaps not as quickly as it would have without printing.[8] As for style, Wærferth had few if any prose models. The Reviser, though, with Wærferth's text before him, could in a sense begin where his predecessor left off, and he probably had other models as well (including Æthelwold's writings?). Whatever his helps, the Reviser exercised more control, achieving both greater clarity and tighter composition. He clarified some passages by altering or adding a single word; from other passages he removed an unnecessarily repetitious word. He united portions of phrases or clauses that Wærferth had divided, and he combined phrases and clauses.

Wærferth's original translation survives only in manuscripts copied a century or more after its time of composition. Two nearly complete ones of the eleventh century — Corpus Christi College, Cambridge 322 (**C**) and British Library, Cotton Otho C.i, vol. 2, fols. 1–137 (**O**) — contain all four books of the *Dialogues*; the late-tenth-century fragment Canterbury Cathedral Add. 25 has parts of a few chapters from Book IV. The sole witness of the revision, fols. 1–54 in Bodleian, Hatton 76 (**H**) from the first half of the eleventh century, contains about three-quarters of Books I and II of the translation.[9] Twenty-two leaves now missing, including three at the end, completed those books, but we have no way of knowing whether the revision ever went further. Hatton 76 continues (fols. 55–67) in the same hand with the unique copy, also wanting leaves, of Ælfric's translation of the *Admonitio ad filium spiritualem* attributed to Basil. Thus manuscripts **C** and **O** share all the material found in **H**; **H** never coincides with the Canterbury fragment.

The present work finds and analyzes the larger linguistic differences between Wærferth's original translation and the revision: differences over (1) the use of parts of speech, (2) repetitions of phrase or clause elements, (3) word order within phrases or clauses, (4) the use of phrases and clauses.[10] The corpus comprises only those passages whose language the Reviser changed, not passages that read the same in both versions of the translation. Even though all the readings come directly from the manuscripts, for convenience page and line numbers refer to Hecht's edition, where the texts of **C** and **H** lie in parallel columns, and **O**'s variants from **C** in a critical apparatus at the foot of each page.[11] Quotations have modern capitalization and punctuation; unless indicated otherwise, word division and the expansion of abbreviations follow Hecht. The Latin that accompanies all examples comes from Adalbert de Vogüé's critical text of the *Dialogues*, cited by book, chapter, and line.[12]

Though Kruisinga long ago pointed out the unique importance of the two versions of the *Dialogues* for the study of Old English syntax, until now only Timmer has investigated, in a book and (afterwards) an article.[13] Much of Timmer's work concerns vocabulary, however: the choice of prepositions, the use of *weorþan* or *beon/wesan* as auxiliaries. Meanwhile other scholars either have focused solely on the syntax of the original translation in manuscripts **C** and **O**,[14] or have drawn selectively on one version or the other for evidence when examining particular features of Old English. So the principal job has remained unfinished: to determine what changes the Reviser made in Wærferth's syntax.

Chapter 1

The Use of Parts of Speech

§1. THE REVISER'S CHANGES that concern the parts of speech normally have the effect of making Wærferth's translation more modern. The Reviser uses

the genitive case rather than the dative of possession (§5);

the dative rather than the instrumental (§6);

the endingless locative rather than another, inflected case (§7);

plural number rather than dual (§8);

a possessive or relative pronoun alone rather than the possessive or relative plus a demonstrative pronoun (§§10–11);

an accusative rather than a dative object, for prepositions and verbs (§§13 and 17);

a prepositional phrase rather than an inflected noun or noun phrase (§14);

either *to* plus infinitive or a participle rather than the simple infinitive (§§18–19);

habban plus past participle rather than a simple verb (§20.*c.*).

Other of the changes show the Reviser's greater care: he insists on concord between subject and verb or pronoun and referent (§§2–3); he supplies unexpressed relative pronouns (§12); and he reduplicates conjunctions or adds *þe* to distinguish them from their corresponding adverbs (e.g., *þa þa* instead of *þa*; *forþam þe*, not *forþam*) (§15). When he substitutes a simple verb for Wærferth's resolved tense with *beon/wesan*, however (e.g., *geheold* for *wæs healdende*, or *astrehton* for *wæron astrehte*), or for Wærferth's auxiliary plus infinitive (e.g., *heolde* for *scolde healdan*), the Reviser leaves the translation less like present-day English than he found it (§§20–21). Typically the Latin does not favor the construction of one version or the other. It supports Wærferth's use of nouns or noun phrases instead of prepositional phrases, though, and his use of simple verbs instead of resolved tenses with *habban*. It also supports the Reviser's dropping unnecessary demonstrative pronouns (§§10–11), as well as his substituting simple verbs for verbal phrases with infinitives.

Concord

§2. Subject and verb do not always agree in number.[1] Once Wærferth takes *(inge)þancas*, "thoughts," as an entity; the Reviser, witnessed by manuscript **H**, considers each thought separately (Hecht 94.22; no Latin):

> **CO**: þurh þa toflowendnysse (toflownesse **O**) þæs ylcan (ilcan **O**) streames *sy (se* **O**) onliht(e) and geþenede (geþæned **O**) þa ingeþancas (þoncas **O**) geleaffulra breosta[2]
>
> **H**: þurh þa toflowennysse þæs ylcan streames *beon* onlihte and geþænede þa *inngeþancas* geleaffulra breosta

At another place, given the singular verb *come* found in the main clause, H's plural verb *cuðon* for the indefinite subject *hwilc man*, "someone," seems inadvertent:

CO: him *hwilc man (hwylc monn* O*)* þe hine ne *cuþe*
     ongen(g) come (34.3)
H: *hwilc man* him ongean *come* þe hine ne *cuðon*
Ln: *quis* illum fortasse *nesciret* (1.4.118)

But compare the well-known sentence, *and þonne* rideð ælc *hys weges mid ðan feo and hyt* motan *habban eall*, from "The Voyages of Ohthere and Wulfstan."[3]

§3. Wærferth also uses *hit* or *þæt* instead of the grammatically appropriate pronoun:

CO: hit se ylca (ilca O) wære (46.24)
H: he se ilca wære
Ln: ipsum esse (1.5.45)

CO: and *gehwylce (gehwelce* O*) wyrte* þe he ær (*def.* O) mid
     stale gewilnode (gewillade O), he him *þæt* mid
     mycelre wynsumnysse sealde (25.15)
H: and *þa wyrta* þe he ær mid stale gewilnode to
     ætbredanne, *þa* he him mid mycelre werednysse
     sealde
Ln: et *holera* quae furto adpetebat auferre, ei cum magna
     dulcedine praebuit (1.3.36)

CO: *þæt* wæron swiðe swearte *men(n)* þæt (þe O) me læd-
     don (89.22)
H: *þa* wæron swiðe swearte *men* þe me læddon
Ln: taetri ualde erant *homines* qui me ducebant (1.12.27)

In the first passage Wærferth's *hit* has the right number but wrong gender; in the second, *þæt* has wrong gender and, in view of the Latin, probably wrong number (also note the strict-

ly plural phrase *gehwilce synne* . . . *beoð* found in Book III of the
Dialogues [244.25]); in the third, *þæt* certainly has wrong
number and gender (cf. §25.*a.* below). When the Reviser once
uses *hit* instead of manuscript **C**'s *se ylca*, manuscript **O** already
has the neuter demonstrative *ðæt* (46.14, where Hecht
mistakenly reported *ðæ* for **O**).

Case

§4. The Reviser substitutes genitive nouns or pronouns for
Wærferth's datives of possession (§5), but datives for
Wærferth's instrumentals (§6). The Reviser also uses endingless locatives instead of datives, instrumentals, or ac-
cusatives (§7). Though none of the changes brings the translation closer to the Latin, all make it more modern. The second
change aligns the translation with Middle English, in which the
instrumental case has virtually disappeared;[4] because of the
first and third changes the translation comes to resemble even
present-day English, whose nouns have only genitive and endingless forms.

§5. A dative corresponds to a genitive or possessive, e.g.,

    CO: [he] onælde (inælde **O**) *þam Godes þeowan (þeowe **O**)*
            þæt mod (101.2)
     H: [he] onælde *þæs Godes þeowes* mod
   Ln: *serui Dei* animum . . . accendit (2.2.10)

    CO: and æfter þon his gemynd he geheold *us* to trymnysse
            (trymnesse **O**) (71.26)
     H: and to *ure* trymminge he syððon geheold his gemynd
   Ln: eiusque post memoriam ad instructionem *nostram* . . .
            retinebat (1.10.12)

Ure may represent either the genitive personal pronoun or a
dative singular feminine form of the possessive adjective,
simplified from **urre*.[5] The revision has the genitive or

possessive eight times, the original translation does so four times,[6] e.g.,

> **CO**: *þæs (þ[ ] O)* nama (noma **O**) wæs Seuerus (88.1)
> **H**: *þam* wæs nama Seuerus
> **Ln**: nomine Seuerus (1.12.3)

But this example suggests that in a thirteenth Wærferth's *þære* represents a dative pronoun, the Reviser's a genitive:

> **CO**: *þære* wæs nama (nomo **O**) U(u)lturnus (14.25)
> **H**: *þære* nama is Uulturnus
> **Ln**: nomine Vulturnum (1.2.18)

The Latin has a genitive or possessive with the revision three times (18.16, 71.26, 101.2) and with Wærferth twice (6.22, 20.9); once it has a dative with Wærferth (79.16), once a dative or (as v.l.) genitive (81.24, quoted in §33.*a.* below).

§6. Elsewhere the dative case supersedes the instrumental.[7]

a. After the prepositions *mid* and *for* the Reviser sometimes replaces the masculine or neuter instrumental singular demonstrative *þy* (v.ll. *ði, ðig*) with dative *þam*. The demonstrative either stands alone in adverb or conjunction formulae — *mid þy (þe), mid þam þe, forðam* (46.29 [om. **C**], 142.11 [*mit ty* **O**], 162.5 [*myt ty* **O**]) — or functions as a definite article, e.g.,

> **CO**: mid *þy* (ði **O**) duste (4.34)
> **H**: mid *þam* duste
> **Ln**: puluere (1.Prologue.27)

The Latin has a conjunction or adverb for the first type of example; for the second, an unambiguously ablative (4.34, 26.31, 38.16, 150.7) or an ablative/dative (9.13) noun or noun phrase. See further §13.*c.* below.

b. An absolute construction once has as its subject the independent instrumental pronoun *ðy* in manuscript **O** of Wærferth's
original translation but the dative *ðysum* in the revision:

> **CO**: þa (*ðy* **O**) gedonum, hit gelamp þæt . . . (169.19)
> **H**: *ðysum* gedonum, hit gelamp þæt . . .
> **Ln**: *quo* facto contigit, ut . . . (2.34.11)

The scribe of manuscript **C** may have written *þa* in error for *þā*,
the abbreviated form of *þam* (cf. **C**'s -*ū* for -*u at 105.17); or
perhaps he intended the adverb *þa*, "then," leaving an absolute
without subject. A later scribe glossed **O**'s *ðy* with *ergo*, constru-
ing that form as an adverb and likewise leaving *gedonum* without
subject. The combination of cases found in **O**, where instrumental subject *ðy* accompanies dative verb *gedonum*, occurs
in two absolute constructions used by the Old English
translator of Bede's *Historia Ecclesiastica*;[8] also compare **C**'s *þam
habbude . . . gangende* (37.14), discussed in §50 below.

c. For the phrase "some day," Wærferth employs the instrumental *sume*, the Reviser the dative *sumon*, phonologically
reduced from *sumum (3.2 [def. **O**], 20.18, 30.29, 80.3). Here
except for manuscript **O**'s one instance of the endingless
locative *dæg* (20.18), both versions always have *dæge*. But in
another passage the revision has *sume dæg* instead of the original
translation's *sume dæge* (57.4, cited again in the next
paragraph).[9] The Latin invariably reads *quadam* or *quodam die*.

§7. The temporal expressions *sume dæg* (57.4), *gyrstandæg*
(39.19), and *todæg* (38.21 [prepositional phrase **C**, *þis ilcan dæge*
O], 85.20, 158.7 [def. **O**]) replace the equivalent dative or instrumental forms in *dæge*, though once the original translation
has the prepositional object *Sæternes dæg* beside the revision's
Sæternes dæge (83.32). *Sume dæg* must represent an endingless
locative, but *gyrstandæg*, *todæg*, and *Sæternes dæg* may serve as ac-
cusatives rather than as locatives.[10] The Latin reads *quodam die,
die hesterno, hodierna die* (38.21), *hodie*, or *sabbato*. For one spatial

expression, the Reviser's hapax legomenon *stocwic* in the locative case corresponds to Wærferth's dative or accusative prepositional object:

> **CO**: in Cassinum þære stowe (þæt stoc **O**) (172.4)
> **H**: on Casino þam stocwic
> **Ln**: in Casinum castrum (2.35.36)

See further §13.*a.* below.

Number

§8. A plural form supersedes the dual personal pronoun or possessive adjective found in the original translation:

> **CO**: awæce (awece **O**) *uncerne* (deadan) broþur (broðor **O**) (84.15)
> **H**: awece *urne* deadan broðor
> **Ln**: ressuscita mortuum *nostrum* (1.10.198)

> **CO**: gewitað inc anweg (onweg **O**) gan and ne secge *git* þis nanum mæn (men **O**), forþon þæt is þæt gyt (git **O**) biddað þæs ælmihtigan Godes hæs (84.20)
> **H**: gewitað incc heonone and ne spreke *ge* þas þing, forþam þe þæt þæt git biddað is þæs ælmihtigan Godes hæs
> **Ln**: recedite et haec dicere nolite, quia iussio omnipotentis Dei est (1.10.200)

Even though the duals *inc(c)* and *gyt* or *git* flank the clause, the Reviser uses *ge* instead of *git* after the shortened present plural imperative verb *spreke* (shortened from **sprekaþ* and replacing *secge*, shortened from **secgaþ*).[11] English dual forms did not survive the thirteenth century.[12]

Pronouns

§9. The Reviser drops otiose demonstrative pronouns, when they accompany possessives (§10) or the indeclinable relative *þe* (§11), yet adds relative pronouns left unexpressed by Wærferth (§12). The first two changes may reduce the translation's emphasis but not its clarity. The third improves clarity, and all three changes bring the translation closer to the Latin.

§10. Wærferth's possessives often have accompanying demonstrative pronouns, e.g.,

> **CO**: *min þæt ungesælige mod* (4.9)
> **H**: *min ungesælige mod*
> **Ln**: infelix . . . animus *meus* (1.Prologue.16)

The Reviser strikes off the demonstrative here and in nine other passages, including one with the possessive *þæs* instead of a personal pronoun or adjective (64.27) and one with the demonstrative *þes* instead of a form of *se* (141.20).[13] The possessive *ure* follows *þes*, and once *his* follows *se* (35.21); otherwise the demonstrative follows the possessive. Having either a possessive alone (4.9, 35.21, 64.27, 141.20, 155.11 [five times]) or no corresponding word, the Latin never supports the original translation.

§11. A demonstrative pronoun likewise falls away before the indeclinable relative *þe*. Only two of Wærferth's demonstratives, however, must belong to the adjective clause and not the main clause:[14]

> **CO**: and eac me byþ ful(l) oft to gemynde becumen and geþeoded to e(a)can mines sares *sum(e)ra manna (monna* **O**) lif, *þa þe* forleton mid eallum (ealle **O**) mode þas andweardan worulde (world **O**) (6.23)
> **H**: soðlice to eacan minum sare foroft me to gemynde becymð *sumra manna* lif, *þe* mid eallum mode forleton þas andweardan woruld

Ln: nonnumquam uero ad augmentum mei doloris
  adiungitur, quod *quorumdam* uita, *qui* praesens
  saeculum tota mente reliquerunt, mihi ad memoriam
  reuocatur (1.Prologue.47)

CO: se *se þe* nolde beon underþeoded (beon[ ]derþeoded
  O) mid hyrsumnysse (hyrsumnesse **O**) to þon þæt he
  agæfe (ageafe **O**) þam halgan were Furtunato his
  cnihtas for heora (hira **O**) weorðe, *se* wæs eft mid
  wite genyded (genided **O**) þæt (. . .) he ageaf(e) hi
  butan ceape (83.1)

  H: se *þe* nolde beon underþeodd hyrsumnysse to þam
  þæt he þa cnapan wið weorðe ageafe þam halgan
  were Furtunate, *se* wearð eft mid wite geneadod þæt
  he hi ageaf butan weorðe

Ln: *qui* sancto uiro Fortunato pueros cum pretio reddere
  oboedientia subiectus noluit, eos sine pretio poena
  subactus daret (1.10.178)

Elsewhere the demonstrative found in just one version of the
translation, usually the original, may form part of the main
clause as the antecedent of *þe*.

§12. The Reviser twice supplies a relative pronoun omitted by
Wærferth:

CO: me lysteþ wel *þæs þu* sagas(t) (20.6)
  H: wel me licað *þæs þe þu* sægst
Ln: libet *quod* dicis (1.2.86)

CO: *he* cym(e)ð æfter me, *se þu* secest (37.11)
  H: *he* cymð nu æfter me, *se þe þu* secst
Ln: *quem* quaeris, ecce subsequitur (1.4.170)

Whether expressed or not, the relative pronoun serves as the
direct, accusative object of the adjective clause. The pronoun's
antecedent, however, *þæs* or *he*, has a different case.[15] When the

Reviser once omits the relative, both it and its antecedent serve
as direct objects:

> **CO**: he ongan (ongon **O**) þa geþenc(e)an æfter þan (ðon
>   **O**) *þa god þe* he ær forleas (106.33)
> **H**: he ongann þa syððon geþencean *þa god* he ær forleas
> **Ln**: postmodum coepit cogitare *bona quae* perdidit (2.3.56)

Here the Latin has both an antecedent and a relative pronoun;
for the first two passages, only a relative.

Prepositions and postpositions

§13. Except for temporal expressions with *in* or *on*, the
revision's prepositional phrases favor accusative rather than
dative objects. The revision's postpositions invariably take
dative objects.[16]

a. Both manuscripts of the original translation show *in* and *on*
freely as preposition and postposition.[17] The Reviser, though,
always chooses *on* for these parts of speech, reserving *in(n)* for
the adverb, usually with *to* or *on* (*in to, in on*). For expressions of
"time when" comprising *in* or *on* (and translating Latin ablative
nouns or noun phrases), Wærferth's accusative prepositional
object corresponds to a dative,[18] e.g.,

> **CO**: in ða ylcan (ilcan **O**) tid (16.6)
> **H**: on þam ylcan timan
> **Ln**: eodem . . . tempore (1.2.37)

The preposition *in* or *on* also has objects of different case to express spatial relations; yet without exception the one version's
accusative can indicate motion toward, the other's dative can
indicate position,[19] e.g.,

> **CO**: Langbearde (Longbearde **O**) foron herg(i)ende in
>   *Ualeria(m) þa mægðe* (42.25)

H: Langbearde foron hergiende on *Ualeria þære ylcan*
        mægðe
Ln: eandem Valeriae prouinciam (*v.l.* prouinciae)
        Langobardis intrantibus (1.4.248)

Both versions share the same meaning, however, when the
postposition has objects of different case:

CO: and (ða giet ða) he *hine* feorran *on* locode (36.16)
H: and he þa gita feorron *him on* locode
Ln: *eum* adhuc longe positus *a*spexit (1.4.155)

CO: þa dryas . . . mid langum onsangum (longum on-
         songum **O**) *hi* golon *on* (73.27)
H: þa dryas þær mid langsumum galdrum *hyre on* golon
Ln: diutinis incantationibus agere malefici moliebantur
         (1.10.41)

CO: se deofol . . . *hi* ær *in* gefor (73.28)
H: se deofol . . . *hyre* ær *on* gefor
Ln: is . . . *eam in*uaserat diabolus (1.10.41)

Most of these particles may represent verbal prefixes rather
than postpositions. Hecht for instance printed *on locode* as one
word, though compare *lociende on me* found in all three
manuscripts, **C**, **O**, and **H**, at 3.34.

b. The preposition *ongean* (v.ll. *ongen, ongæn*) sometimes takes a
dative object in Wærferth's original translation, an accusative
in the revision, e.g.,

CO: þa worhte (awrat **O**) he sylf Cristes rodetacen mid his
         fin(c)grum *ongen þam gledum* (87.15)
H: þa worhte he Cristes rodetaken mid his fingrum
         ongean þa gledu
Ln: signum crucis digito *contra prunas (v.l., in Moricca,*
         pruna) fecit (1.11.11)

Otherwise (17.16, 37.6) the Latin does not have a prepositional phrase. When in a fourth example the versions have the opposite cases, the Reviser uses *ongean* as a postposition or verbal prefix (156.11, Latin *contra se* [2.25.8]; see further §37.*b.* below).

c. On two or three occasions the object of *mid* has a different case:[20]

> **CO**: heora (hiora **O**) hors *mid swa hræde ryne* þa ea oferfer-
> don (15.30)
> **H**: hyra hors þa *mid swa hrædlicum ryne* oferferdon þa ea
> **Ln**: quorum equi tanto cursu illum . . . fluuium trans-
> ierunt (1.2.32)

> **CO**: (se hlaf) . . . wæs gemeted (and) gemearcod *mid
> Cristes rodetacne* (87.22)
> **H**: se hlaf . . . wæs . . . gemeted gemearcod *mid Cristes
> rodetacen*
> **Ln**: qui . . . cruce signatus inuentus est (1.11.14)

> **C**: and *hine mid* siðian seo mænigeo þara þegniendra
> manna (131.22)
> **O**: and hine mid soðe sio mænigio þara þenindra monna
> **H**: and *him mid* siðode micel meniu þeniendra manna
> **Ln**: obsequentum frequentia comitatus (2.14.17)

Wærferth's *hræde ryne* may represent an accusative plural or an instrumental singular; compare

> **CO**: he . . . eft mid færlicum (færlice **O**) ryne gecyrde
> (gecirde **O**) (115.21)
> **H**: he . . . mid swiftum ryne eft gecyrde
> **Ln**: rapido . . . cursu rediit (2.7.16)

CO: mid hrædlicum ryne (hrædlice yrne **O**) he fleah
   (278.15)
Ln: cursu concito . . . fugit (4.13.31)

See further §6.*a.* above.

d. The Reviser sometimes replaces *fore*, "because of, on account
of," with *for* while keeping the same prepositional object (51.21,
58.22 [om. **C**], 157.33 [def. **O**]). Another time he changes the
object's case and leaves the preposition untouched:

CO: he mid his gebedum *for his synnum* þingode (88.10)
 H: he . . . mid his gebedum þingode *for his synna*
Ln: suisque orationibus *pro peccatis eius* intercederet
   (1.12.7)

Once he changes both particle and object (see Wende, *Präpositionen*, p. 14, and also §37.*b.* below):

CO: he *for (om.* **O***) hine* gebæde (38.1)
 H: he *him fore* gebæde
Ln: orationem *pro se* fieri (1.4.180)

This last quotation from manuscript **H** perhaps exemplifies the
verb *foregebiddan*, "to intercede," used by Æthelwold.[21]

e. The preposition *beforan* on two occasions certainly has a
dative plural object in the original translation but has either a
dative singular or an accusative plural in the revision:

CO: eall þes middaneard (middan[ ]rd **O**) . . . wære
   gegaderod (gegeagrad **O**) and gelæded *beforan his
   eagum* (171.14)
 H: eall middaneard . . . gelogod wære *beforan his eagan*
   gelæded
Ln: omnis etiam mundus, . . . collectus, *ante oculos eius*
   adductus est (2.35.25)

CO: *beforan his eagum* . . . eall middan(g)eard wære
      gegaderod (172.23)
 H: *beforan his eagan* . . . eall middaneard wære gegaderod
Ln: *ante oculos ipsius* . . . omnis mundus adductus est
      (2.35.45)

Harting apparently would construe *eagan* as accusative (pp. 288–89).

f. The object that the Reviser supplies for *buton* allows even more choice:

CO: buton earfoðnyssum (butan earfeðnessum **O**) (174.7)
 H: buton earfoðnysse
Ln: sine difficultate (2.35.67)

Dative singular, accusative singular, or accusative plural? Does *earfoðnysse* take its number from the original translation or from the Latin?

§14. One of the revision's most striking modern features, the use of prepositional or (twice) postpositional phrases in place of Wærferth's substantives or substantive phrases, comprehends sixteen or seventeen particles and all five major cases.[22] Here a prepositional phrase with *mid* supplants an instrumental noun phrase:

CO: þonne wæron hi forðbroht(e) *ceorlisc(r)e ðeawe* (9.16)
 H: þonne wæron hy forðbrohte *mid cyrlisceum þeawe*
Ln: haec *rusticano usu* prolata (1.Prologue.90)

The table (p. 27) indicates the equivalences that occur, the top "X" for instance meaning that (on at least one occasion) a dative, instrumental, or locative substantive or substantive phrase corresponds to a prepositional or postpositional phrase

Table.
Prepositional and postpositional phrases corresponding to
substantives or substantive phrases of various cases.

	nominative	genitive	genitive or dative?	dative, instrumental or locative	accusative
æfter				x	
æt			x		
be		x			x
for	x		x	x	
fram			x	x	
geond				x	
in, on	x	x	x	x	x
mid		x		x	
of	x		x	x	
ofer				x	
ongean				x	
þurh		x		x	
to	x			x	x
under				x	
wið				x	
ymb(e)				x	x

with *æfter*. Of all the examples, though, only two involve postpositions: *him sylfum* **C**, *him seolfum* **O**, *him to* **H** (35.3) and *ham* **CO**, *ham ongean* **H** (89.33). As for the prepositions, all but one of them immediately precedes its object: **H**'s *on . . . þam*, replacing **CO**'s simple *þam* (63.18). Neither the table nor the following discussion includes those passages in which a preposition corresponds to a postposition or verbal prefix, e.g.,

> **CO**: þa gyfa (gife **O**) gaþ (nu) *beforan* ælcum weorce (33.9)
> **H**: þa gifa *fore*stæppað ælc weorc
> **Ln**: opus dona *prae*ueniunt (1.4.105)

> **C**: geongran mæn sacerdhad underfengon (135.26)
> **O**: gingran þonne he wære wæron him seolfum *ofer*gesette in þam halgum sacerdhadum
> **H**: his gingran wæron *toforan* him gesette on halgum sacerdhadum
> **Ln**: minores suos sibimet *super*poni in sacris ordinibus (2.16.17)

See further §37.*b.* below.

a. Wærferth (*on* 79.16) or the Reviser (*for* 22.3, 22.4, 118.6; *of* 46.9; *to* 157.25) uses a prepositional phrase when the other uses a noun or noun phrase of the nominative case, e.g.,

> **CO**: hit *his sylfes gylt* wære swiðor þonne hit *ðæs abbudes uncysta* wæron (22.3–4)
> **H**: hit wære *for his agenum gylte* . . . and na *for þæs abbodes reðnysse*
> **Ln**: *suae culpae*, non *illius saeuitiae* fuisse (1.2.115)

The Latin has genitive noun phrases here, a nominative noun at 157.25; otherwise it has prepositional phrases with the revision or (79.16) an incomparable construction.

b. Wærferth's genitives also succumb to prepositional phrases, governed by *be* (32.30), *on* (27.27), and *þurh* (17.32 [instrumental **O**],46.22, 77.23, 81.9 [instrumental **O**]). Sometimes the Latin has a substantive or substantive phrase (17.32, 27.27, 77.23 [quoted at the end of §33.*b.* below], 81.9), sometimes a prepositional phrase (32.30, 46.22). The Reviser once substitutes *his* for *mid him*:

> **CO:** þa wæs þær sum munuc (munoc **O**) *mid him* se wæs
> sumes rices mannes (mones **O**) sunu (143.31)
> **H:** þa wæs *his* an munuc sumes gerefan sunu
> **Ln:** *eius* monachus cuiusdam defensoris filius fuerat
> (2.20.2)

Another time, however, he replaces Wærferth's genitive noun phrase with both a prepositional phrase and the possessive *hyra*:

> **CO:** hi symble æfæstiað (æfestigeað **O**) *oþ(e)ra manna (mon-*
> *na* **O**) goddæde (goddæda **O**) and hefelice niþas
> (hefiglice niðað **O**) (117.4)
> **H:** hi æfstiað *on oðrum mannum hyra* mægenes god
> **Ln:** inuidere *aliis (v.l. in aliis)* uirtutis bonum (2.8.5)

Because of manuscript **O**'s readings two of the examples come up again in the paragraph after next (17.32, 81.9).

c. Almost a dozen noun phrases may exhibit either the genitive or the dative case, e.g.,

> **CO:** þa landleode (landliode **O**) *on (in* **O**) þære stowe* (97.32)
> **H:** *þære stowe* landleodan
> **Ln:** *eius loci* incolae (2.1.21)

The Latin shares nouns or noun phrases with the original translation or (33.16, 33.17, 97.32) revision, shares prepositional phrases with the revision (26.29, 95.11, 151.1), or does not support either version (75.28, 76.17: the Reviser uses the prepositional phrase). The prepositions include *æt* (75.28, 76.17), *for* (61.7, 61.9), *fram* (26.29, 151.1), *in* or *on* (33.16, 33.17, 97.32, 137.4; cf. 117.13 quoted in note 27 below), and *of* (95.11).

d. Wærferth's dative, instrumental, or locative phrase often corresponds to the Reviser's prepositional or (35.3, 89.33) postpositional phrase. Not infrequently, though, the writers use the opposite constructions.[23] The substantives serve as

> indirect objects (*fram* 97.29; *mid* 75.3; *on* 63.18; *to* 35.3, 81.33, 95.3, 103.33, 152.10 [five times]; *wið* 21.32),

> temporal expressions (*on* [nineteen times];[24] *to* 74.16 [accusative **C**]),

> spatial expressions[25] (*fram* 15.29; *geond* 101.19; *of* 26.26; *ofer* 173.11; *on* 56.28; *ongean* 89.33 [but see note 27 below]; *ymb* 131.13 [def. **O**]),

> expressions of manner or means (*mid* 9.16 [quoted at the beginning of this section], 56.11, 74.2, 74.3, 83.2, 164.11 [six times]; *of* 41.26; *þurh* [genitive **C**] 17.32, 81.9),

> expressions of reason or cause (*for* 9.1 [om. **C**], 55.25, 136.11, 145.20, 152.14 [five times]), and

> dative absolutes[26] (*æfter* 53.10; *mid* 118.27[twice]; *þurh* 94.15; *under* 52.4).

One of the examples recurs in the next paragraph because of manuscript **C**'s reading (74.16); two others have already appeared in paragraph *b.* above (17.32, 81.9). The Latin has a substantive or substantive phrase about four-fifths of the time and thus usually parallels the original translation.

e. Prepositional phrases twice replace Wærferth's direct objects (*on* 117.13; *ymbe* 4.19 [def. **O**]).[27] On no less than five occasions, however, the Reviser uses the direct object (*be* 127.26; *on* 131.25, 148.18; *to* 80.30, 170.33). The Reviser also substitutes a prepositional phrase for Wærferth's accusative of time (*on* 52.18; *to* 74.16 [**O** has a dative: see the above paragraph]); yet just as often the original translation retains a prepositional phrase instead of an accusative of extent (*in* 114.34)[28] or adverbial *hwæt* (*to* 40.20). For all but the penultimate example (114.34), for which it has a prepositional phrase, the Latin has a substantive or substantive phrase.

Adverbs and conjunctions

§15. To distinguish a relative adverb or a conjunction from the simple adverb, the Reviser will reduplicate the form or add the indeclinable particle *þe*,[29] e.g.,

> **CO**: hi(g) hit geleornodon (geleornedon **O**) *swa* hi hit gehyrdon (9.2)
> **H**: hi hit geleornodon *swa swa* hi hit gehyrdon
> **Ln**: auditu didicerunt (1.Prologue.84)

> **CO**: ic eom nu geslægen (slegen **O**) *forþon (forðam* **O***)* he me wyrgde (82.9)
> **H**: ic eom nu geslagen *forþam þe* he me wyrigde
> **Ln**: *quia* maledixisti mihi, ecce percussus sum (1.10.166)

Twice in short succession (108.31, 109.2) the relative adverb "where" appears as *þær þær* rather than as *þær* (**O**) or *þær þe* (**C**). The conjunctions *swa* (9.2, 24.18, 34.26, 35.12, 44.15 [five times]) and *þa,* "when," likewise reduplicate.[30] Although the revision twice has *swa* instead of the original translation's *swa swa* (148.26, 172.26), on two other occasions *swa mycel* expands to *swa mycel swa* (41.18, 100.26). The Reviser adds *þe* to the relative adverb *þanon* (59.27), and to the conjunctions *þy læs* (*þe læs þe* 35.26, 50.20, 80.33, 128.17) and *forþon* or *forþam.*[31] Once, however, *forþon* or *forþam þe* loses its particle *þe* (45.1), and once *þe(a)h þe* does so (34.2). Finally in two examples the revision has the simple conjunction *þæt* instead of the original translation's *þætte*, from *þæt þe (7.15, 139.19 [om. **C**]).[32]

Verbs

§16. Some verbs get an accusative object in place of the dative found in the original translation (§17). Rather than the simple infinitive, the Reviser uses either *to* plus inflected infinitive (§18) or a participle (§19); rather than a resolved tense with participle (§20) or infinitive (§21), he uses a simple verb.

§17. "The dative is the case of . . . the indirect object, but in O[ld] E[nglish] . . . the dative is also used in a function which obviously does not differ much from that of the direct object. In many cases of this kind, however, the dative begins to be superseded by the accusative even in O[ld] E[nglish], the instances in which the dative survives beyond early M[iddle] E[nglish] being comparatively few in number."[33] Some passages from the translation of the *Dialogues* exemplify Mustanoja's next to last contention:

> **CO**: *þam* he sylf(a) mihte (meahte **O**) uneaðe *gewyldan* (*gewealdan* **O**) (36.6)
> **H**: *þone* he sylf uneaðe mihte *gewyldan*
> **Ln**: *cui* uix poterat uel ipse *dominari* (1.4.150)

> **CO**: his gecorenan *fylgeað þære bysene* (61.1)
> **H**: his gecorenan *fylgeað þa gebysnunga*
> **Ln**: electi eius, *exempla* (*v. ll. exemplum, exemplo*) . . . *sequentes* (1.9.71)

> **CO**: se ealda feond *onfeng swylcere bylde (swelcere byldo **O**)* to acwyllane (cwe[ ]lanne **O**) (75.33)
> **H**: se ealda feond *onfeng swilce dyrstinysse* to acwellanne
> **Ln**: occidendi *ausum* . . . antiquus hostis *acceperit* (1.10.72)

The Reviser also uses *underfon* with an accusative instead of Wærferth's *onfon* with a dative (118.8), and *gehyran* with an accusative once replaces *hyran* with dative (80.31).

§18. The auxiliary *gewunode* governs Wærferth's simple infinitive but the Reviser's infinitive phrase:[34]

> **CO**: hit ne *gewunode* naht (noht **O**) elles *penc(e)an* (4.18)
> **H**: hit ne *gewunode* nan þing elles *to þenceanne*
> **Ln**: nulla . . . *cogitare consueuerat* (1.Prologue.20)

Otherwise whenever one version has a simple infinitive and the other *to* plus inflected infinitive, then the auxiliaries, the infinitives, or both differ: e.g., the Reviser once uses *ferde to hladene* instead of Wærferth's *eode . . . hladan* (115.6), once *ongann . . . to þancienne* instead of *ongan . . . don . . . þancas* (38.4). The only current relic of the verb *(ge)wunian*, the adjective "wont" from past participle *wunod*, takes "to" with infinitive.

§19. After the verb *gemette* a transitive past participle *bepæhte*, "deceived," replaces the intransitive infinitive *bysmrian*, "blaspheme":[35]

> **CO**: þa broðru . . . þe he *gemette* þær mid þam (ðy **O**)
> scinlacan fyre *bysmrian* (124.11)
> **H**: þa broðru þe he *gemette* mid þam gedwimorlicum fyre
> *bepæhte*
> **Ln**: eos quos phantastico *repperit* igne *deludi (v.l. deludere)*
> (2.10.11)

Perhaps each Old English writer merely followed the reading of his particular Latin exemplar, Wærferth translating *deludere*, the Reviser *deludi*. Present-day English would require a participle for "met": either transitive "deceived" or intransitive "blasphem*ing*."

§20. Rather than fall in with the (ultimate) English trend toward resolved tenses with "to be" plus participle, the Reviser, sometimes despite the Latin, employs single verbs. Yet he does choose to introduce resolved tenses made up of a form of *habban* plus past participle.

a. Wærferth's verbal phrase consisting of a form of *beon/wesan* plus present participle corresponds to the Reviser's simple finite verb,[36] e.g.,

> **CO**: þu oferfærest þone sæ and *bist gangende* (ofer[ ]ang-
>   ende **O**) to Rome(s)byrig (132.31)
>   **H**: witodlice in to Rome þu *becymst*; ofer sæ þu færst
> **Ln**: Romam *ingressurus es*, mare transiturus (2.15.10)

The Latin parallels the original translation here. Everywhere else both versions have preterite verbs (e.g., *wæs gangende, eode*) and the Latin does not agree exactly with either, having the deponent *testatur* (110.5),[37] a perfect infinitive (30.20, def. **O**), a participle alone,[38] or a perfect participle with a form of *sum*.[39]

b. The Reviser also substitutes a simple finite verb for Wærferth's form of *beon/wesan* with past participle, though twice the versions have the opposite constructions:[40]

> **CO**: ne *cym(e)ð* naht (noht **O**) ungelic trymnes upp (8.1)
>   **H**: swiðe gelic trymming *byð upsprungen*
> **Ln**: non dispar aedificatio *oritur* (1.Prologue.69)

> **CO**: se halga fæder in þone (ilcan) wyrt(t)un *ineode* (31.11)
>   **H**: se halga fæder *wæs inn agan* on þone wyrttun
> **Ln**: hortum isdem pater *ingressus est (v.l. ingressus)* (1.4.77)

The Latin sometimes encourages the resolved tense by having a (present) form of *sum* with perfect participle (31.11, 81.27, 132.3, 148.29 [**O** has a present participle: see note 39 above], 149.18 [five times]). Otherwise it has a single verb form: a present passive finite verb (6.20, 8.1), an imperfect passive (154.29), a perfect participle (31.11 [as v.l.], 130.2). On two other occasions the Reviser uses a form of *weorþan* with a past participle:

CO: he . . . beot Libertinum on þæt heafod and on þa onsyne oþ þæt he gedyde þæt eall his andwlita (ondwlita **O**) *awannode and asweol(l)* (20.32)

H: he . . . beot Libertinum on þæt heafod and on þa ansyne oð þæt eall his andwlita *wearð toswollen and awannod*

Ln: ei caput ac faciem tutundit totumque illius uultum tumentum ac liuidum reddidit (1.2.96)

CO: he wæs wundriende þa wisan and *(a)forhtode* (115.29)

H: þa *wearð* he mid wundrunge *afyrht* for þære dæde

Ln: miratus *extremuit (v.l. expauit)* factum (2.7.19)

All the above examples differ from the nearly fifty in which one version has a passive and the other version an active expression, e.g.,

CO: þu ne þurfe me tyðian (tiðian **O**) þæs þe *þu gebeden (g)eart* (28.9)

H: þu ne þurfe getiðian þæs þe *ic þe bidde*

Ln: ne debeas praestare quod *peteris (v.l. peto)* (1.4.32)

The former show the same subject in each version accompanying an intransitive verb (e.g., *(a)forhtian* or *afyrhtan*); the latter have a transitive verb (e.g., *biddan*), hence different subjects (*ic*, *þu*).[41]

c. Whenever a form of *habban* plus past participle corresponds to a single verb, normally the Reviser not Wærferth uses the resolved tense.[42] Wærferth retains *habban* only when confronted with the cognate *habere*—

CO: hwæt he unrihtes ([ ]rihtes **O**) *gedon hæfde oððe geþoht*
in his heortan (i[ ] **O**) (144.24)
H: hwæt he on his heortan *smeade*
Ln: quid *habuerit* in corde (2.20.15)

— or when the Reviser imitates the Latin's absolute construction (59.8, quoted in §50 below). Otherwise the Latin has either a finite verb (not *habere*: 25.6, 90.2, 143.14), an infinitive (60.19), or a participle (143.13). The Old English also has infinitives at 60.19, where *habban forsuwod* replaces *forswigian*.

§21. Wærferth's verbal phrase of auxiliary plus infinitive often corresponds to a simple finite verb,[43] e.g.,

CO: hwylc æfter þam *beon sceolde* (147.26)
H: hwylc *wære* æfter oðrum
Ln: quis eis secundus *esset* (2.22.5)

The auxiliaries include *sceolan, willan* or *nellan, magan, onginnan, lætan, *motan*, and **durran*, all of which take an uninflected infinitive. Two other auxiliaries, *geteohhian* and *gewunian*, occurring in the revision, take *to* with inflected infinitive. By generally having the auxiliary the original translation agrees with present-day English. It seems likely, though, that the Reviser led himself away from the modern path only because he chose for the most part to adopt the construction found in the Latin.

a. Wærferth uses the form of *sceolan* with infinitive fourteen of fifteen times (not at 131.16). Six of the verbs opposite *sceolan*, in the other version, must represent subjunctives (39.16, 46.27, 54.23, 57.23, 131.16, 147.26 [quoted above]); three, indicatives (56.27, 62.19, 118.12). The rest may exhibit either mood (38.10, 58.2, 59.26, 104.12, 131.9 [def. **O**], 131.12 [six times]).[44] The Latin has the phrases *fatigari debeatis* (39.16), *praeparari faceret* (58.2), and *esse . . . simulantes* (131.9); otherwise only single or (46.27) no verb forms. The three Old English phrases with *sceolan* in the present tense could indicate future time (39.16, 54.23, 62.19; see Wattie, "Tense," p. 129).

b. Except at 81.5 the auxiliary *willan* or *nellan* appears in the original translation. The other version's simple finite verb has the imperative (80.32, 88.34 [quoted in note 41 above]), the subjunctive (81.10, 148.27), the indicative (43.3, 69.2, 76.25), or an uncertain, either subjunctive or indicative (42.19, 81.5, 124.20, 127.24, 128.21, 154.22, 155.31 [seven times]), mood. A Latin auxiliary *noli* turns up, plus infinitive, only for the imperatives. Six of the examples, with their verbs of the present tense, may involve future time (42.19, 43.3, 76.25, 80.32, 88.34, 128.21; see Wattie, "Tense," p. 130).

c. Wærferth (8.7, 35.10, 73.5, 163.13) and the Reviser (37.28, 75.13, 136.23, 148.10) each use the auxiliary *magan*: three times opposite a subjunctive verb, three times opposite an indicative (8.7, 75.13, 136.23 [but see note 40 above]), and twice opposite a verb of ambiguous mood (37.28, 148.10). The Latin has *uenire potuissent* for the passage at 148.10, no auxiliary for the others.

d. The Reviser's simple finite verbs, of uncertain mood, also correspond to phrases comprising a form of *onginnan* with infinitive. The Latin once has *curauit indicare* (114.8), once *conatus est* (130.26, om. **C**), and twice a single verb form (32.18, 123.30). On a fifth occasion, *ongunnon . . . þeahtian* replaces Wærferth's *(ge)eodon . . . in geþeaht* (74.7, Latin *inito consilio* [1.10.46]; cf. 104.28 quoted at the end of §50 below).

e. A few phrases include the auxiliaries *lætan* (35.8, 132.29 [def. **O**]), **motan* (27.27), or **durran* (39.9). Wærferth uses *moste beon*, the Reviser *dorste geþristlæcean*, and each writer *læt* with an infinitive. The verbs opposite *læt* have the imperative and (35.8) subjunctive moods; the verb opposite *moste* has the subjunctive; the verb opposite *dorste* has the indicative or subjunctive. The Latin possesses only single verb forms.

f. Unlike the other auxiliaries, *geteohhian* (96.20) and *gewunian* (64.9, 125.27, 157.19) accompany *to* with inflected infinitive (see §18 above) and occur only in the revision. But again the Reviser follows the Latin, which has the corresponding auxiliaries *consueuerat* and (96.20) *decreuisset*.

Chapter 2

Repetitions of Phrase or Clause Elements

§22. THE REVISER DOES AWAY with many unnecessary repetitions: of dependent demonstratives or possessives, subjects, objects, conjunctions, and auxiliary verbs. The deletions usually bring the Old English into agreement with the Latin. Despite the Latin, however, the Reviser will on occasion repeat a preposition found only once in the original translation.

Dependent demonstrative pronoun or possessive

§23. Each of two parallel adjective or noun phrases joined by *and* may have a demonstrative or possessive,[1] e.g.,

> **CO**: *þam* godum and *þam* geleaffullum werum (weron **O**) (7.24)
>
> **H**: *þam* godum and geleafullum werum
>
> **Ln**: uel bonis ac fidelibus uiris (1.Prologue.64)

> **CO**: *his sylfes (seolfes* **O***)* reðnysse (reðnesse **O**) and *his agene* heardnysse (heardnesse **O**) (21.24)
>
> **H**: *his agene* reðnysse and heardnysse
>
> **Ln**: asperitatem et duritiam *suam* (1.2.109)

For each of two other passages resembling the latter the Latin again has only one possessive (89.24, 95.27).

Subject

§24. The Reviser chooses not to repeat Wærferth's subject in three situations, e.g.,

   CO: *Dauid*, þe gewunade (gewunode **O**) þæt he hæfde
        witedomes gast in him, *he* demde dom ongen . . .
        Ionathanes sunu (40.25)
    H: *Dauid*, þe gewunode to hæbbenne witedomes gast on
        him, demde dom ongean . . . Ionathes sunu
   Ln: *Dauid*, qui prophetiae spiritum habere consueuerat,
        contra . . . Ionathae filium sententiam dedit
        (1.4.222)

   CO: nis *hit* hwæþre to gelyfanne *þæt he þa stowa (stowe **O***)
        forlure (85.28)
    H: swa þeah nis na to gelyfenne *þæt he forlure þa stowe*
   Ln: nec tamen credendum est *quia locum . . . perdidit*
        (1.10.220)

   CO: witodlice *se hælend* worhte þæt wundor, and *he* het hit
        helan (60.31)
    H: witodlice *se hælend* worhte þæt wundor and het hi
        helan
   Ln: miraculum namque faciens, et taceri (*v.l.* tacere)
        iussit (1.9.70)

Though both versions of the translation have basically the same word order, at 40.25 Wærferth reiterates the subject after the intrusion of a dependent (adjective) clause. At 85.28 the pronoun *hit* anticipates a noun *þæt*-clause. Finally at 60.31 the subject appears in each of two clauses joined by *and*.

a. Wærferth repeats the subject when an adjective or (59.33) adverb clause intervenes before the completion of the main clause. The subject appears first as a noun phrase (52.1, 129.27, 142.33 [def. **O**]), name (40.25), or demonstrative pronoun (54.8, 55.1, 59.33); then, after the dependent clause, as a personal or (52.1, 129.27) demonstrative pronoun. The Latin like the revision expresses the subject only once.

b. When a noun *þæt*-clause serves as a subject, Wærferth or (63.15, om. **O**) the Reviser makes its role clear by means of a preceding pronoun *hit* or (172.12, def.**O**) *þæt*. About half the time the Latin has only a *quia*- (55.14, 63.15, 85.28) or *ut*-clause (15.35, 22.6, 172.12 [as v.l.]); the rest of the time neither a noun clause nor a pronoun (19.15, 27.14, 32.34, 106.34, 117.3, 131.16, 140.34 [seven times]).

c. The Old English writers also differ over the repetition of a subject in the second of two clauses joined by *and* (cf. the passages discussed in §27.*b.* below). Wærferth repeats the initial clause's noun phrase (16.15, 60.31, 64.12, 125.3, 135.32, 141.1 [six times]), name (22.1), or third person personal pronoun (19.12 [om. **O**], 31.23, 65.19 [**O** omits *and*], 95.10, 142.7 [five times]) by means of a personal or (135.32) demonstrative pronoun. The Reviser meanwhile repeats a first person pronoun *ic* (56.11, 155.19) or *we* (106.19). On yet another occasion Wærferth repeats *ic*, but the Reviser expresses *he* only in the first of the two clauses (109.23). When *ac* joins the clauses (125.22), or when the Reviser uses *ac* (124.5) or *ge* (78.26) instead of Wærferth's *and*, again the Reviser not Wærferth repeats the subject. Aside from the passage for which it reads *Langobardi . . . qui* without an intervening conjunction (141.1), the Latin expresses the subject either once or not at all.

Object

§25. The three categories distinguished in §24 for subjects also apply to the repetition of an object. As before, the discussion includes only those passages with essentially the same word order in both versions of the translation, e.g.,

CO: *þære sawle* þe gesyhð (gesihð **O**) hire scyppend þynceð

(þinceð **O**) swiþe nearu (nearo **O**) ælc gesceaft
(173.1)
H: *þære sawle* þe gesihð hyre scyppend, *hyre* þinceð nearo
and lytel ælc gesceaft
Ln: *animae* uidenti creatorem angusta est omnis creatura
(2.35.51)

CO: and þu *þæt* miht eac oncnawan, *þæt (eac) Eliseus mihte
(meahte* **O***) sona þæt mæg(e)n his lareowes (lareawes* **O***)
gegearwi(ge)an* (19.31)
H: and eac þu miht oncnawan *þæt Heliseus mihte sona
begitan his lareowes mægen*
Ln: tunc exhibere magistri uirtutem potuit (1.2.82)

CO: he þa sona sænde (sende **O**) *þa cnihtas* ham . . . and
bead *hi(e)* þam arwyrðan (arwurðam **O**) were Furtunato (81.31)
H: and he þa ofstlice ofsennde and ongean gelædde *þa
cnapan* . . . and asende to þam arwurðan were Furtunate
Ln: qui festinus misit et *pueros* . . . reduxit, et uiro
uenerabili Fortunato mandauit (1.10.160)

a. At 173.1 the Reviser reiterates the dative phrase *þære sawle* by
means of the pronoun *hyre* of the same case. Another time,
again contrary to the Latin, he uses the indefinite accusative *hit*
to refer back to a dative object *þam mode* (35.12; see §3 above).

b. At 19.31 quoted above, Wærferth's pronoun *þæt* anticipates
the noun-clause object of *oncnawan.* The conjunction *þæt*
governs this object clause and five others, but *æt hwilcum* and *hu*
also govern object clauses (9.8, 144.25). On one occasion
Wærferth's pronoun follows a clause governed by the generaliz-
ing relative *swa hwæt swa*:

CO: *swa hwæt swa þu elles bebeodest,* we syndon gearwe (we
ðe wæron[ ] **O**) *þæt* to don(n)e (80.25)

H: we syndon gearwe to donne *swa hwæt swa þu elles bebydst*

Ln: *quicquid aliud praecipis* facere parati sumus (1.10.141)

And once *hit* follows an adverb clause:[2]

CO: hi him mid heora mode oncleofiað (onclifiað **O**) and onclifi(g)ende . . . , *swa swyðe (swiðe **O**) swa hi æt Gode onfoð*, hi *hit* ongytað (ongitað **O**) (139.2)

  H: hi mid hyra mode him onclifiað and onclifiende oncnawað *swa swiðe swa hi onfoð* . . .

Ln: uero ei mente inhaerent, atque inhaerendo . . . , *in quantum accipiunt*, agnoscunt (2.16.66)

Pope has drawn attention to a similar example in Ælfric, *swa swa wisceras oft doð, and bedyriað menn swilce hi soðlice swylc þing don*, commenting that "the antecedent of *swylc* is indefinite" (*Homilies*, 2:797). The Latin parallels the revision seven times, having only a clause governed by *quanto* (144.25, def. **O**) or *in quantum* (139.2), *quibus* (9.8), *quicquid* (80.25), or *quod* (29.9, 38.5, 150.2); twice does not have either a clause or pronoun (19.31, 138.8); and once supports both versions, when the original translation's *þæt* and the Reviser's *him* each translate *hoc* preceding an *ut*-clause (35.24).

c. After the conjunction *and* Wærferth repeats noun-phrase direct objects by means of the personal pronouns *hine* (169.16), *hit* (60.31, quoted at the beginning of §24), and *hi(e)* (81.31, quoted at the begining of this section). The Reviser uses *hine* likewise (18.25, 155.11), and also reiterates the personal pronouns *þe* and *inc* by means of *þe* and *eow* respectively (129.32, 149.11). The Latin invariably has only one object.

Preposition

§26. A preposition may reappear either after *and*, e.g.,

CO: *mid* þegnungum (þeningum **O**) and gewinnum
(102.31)
H: *mid* þenungum and *mid* geswinceum
Ln: obsequiis laboribusque (2.2.38)

(so 20.9, with *to*, and 169.13, with *on*),[3] or in the second of two
appositional phrases:

CO: witodlice se halga wer Benedictus ongan (ongon **O**)
þis wundor tellan nalles na (nallæs no *on* **O**) his
agnum geearnungum ac Maures (Maurus **O**) hyrsumnysse (gehyrsumnesse **O**) þæs muneces (115.33)
H: se arwurða wer Benedictus þa ongann tellan þis wundor *to* Maures hyrsumnysse, na *to* his agenum geearnungum
Ln: uir autem uenerabilis Benedictus hoc non suis
meritis, sed oboedientiae illius deputare coepit
(2.7.21)

Here the Reviser transposes the phrases and dispenses with
Wærferth's coordinating conjunction *ac*. The Latin has either
one preposition, like the original translation (20.9, 169.13), or
none.

Conjunction

§27. *a*. In the middle of a lengthy *þæt*-clause Wærferth tries to
keep the reader oriented by repeating the conjunction:

CO: he ongæt (ongeat **O**) *þæt* þy ylcan (þi i[ ] **O**) niht(e)
þe him se ærendraca æfter wæs sænded (wæs æfter
sended **O**), *þæt* se apostolica bisc(e)op wæs swiðe
abreged on swefne þurh nihtlice gesihþe (39.4)
H: þa sæde he him *þæt* on þære ylcan nyhte þe he se
ærendraca him æfter asended wæs, se healica papa
wearð þurh nihtlice gesihþe on swefne swiðe gebreged

Ln: cognouit *quia* nocte eadem, qua (*v.l.* quia) ipse illuc
executor missus est, per uisum pontifex fuerat
uehementer exterritus (1.4.198)

At 59.22, quoted in §43 below, only manuscript **C** repeats the
conjunction. Also compare the passages of §25.*b.*, in which the
object pronoun *þæt* refers ahead to a *þæt*-clause.

b. The conjunction *þæt* may begin each of two clauses joined by
and, e.g.,

CO: he onbead þam æ(w)fæstan were Theoprobo
(Theopropo **O**) (þæt), *þæt* he onsænde (onsende **O**)
þære ylcan niht (neahte **O**) man to Capuanan þære
byrig and *þæt* he sylf ongeate (ongyte **O**) and eft (*def.*
O) þider gebude hwæt (het **O**) geworden wære
(172.7)

H: [he] þam eawfæstan were Theoprobo þær rihte
bebead *þæt* he on þære ylcan nihte asende sumne
mann to Capuanan þære byri and gewiste and him
eft gecyðde hwæt wære geworden

Ln: religioso uiro Theopropo mandauit, *ut* ad Capuanam
urbem sub eadem nocte transmitteret, et quid . . .
ageretur agnosceret et indicaret (2.35.37)

The subject, here *he*, likewise fails to reappear after *and* (compare §24.*c.* above). The Latin has either one conjunction, *ut*
(60.25 [quoted in §28.*b.*], 131.8, 148.32, 172.7), or none
(102.29, where the Reviser repeats conjunction and subject).

Auxiliary verb

§28. *a.* Wærferth uses a form of the auxiliary *beon/wesan* with
each of two participles (15.2, 173.9) or two adjectives (137.26)
connected by *and*, e.g.,

CO: hi(e) mid þam swipum geswungene *wæron* and mid

þam spurum geblodgode (geblodegade **O**) *wæron*
(15.2)
H: þa hors *wæron* mid swipum swiðe geswungene and
mid þam spurum mistucode
Ln: equi uerberibus caesi, calcaribus cruentati (1.2.20)

When the phrases on either side of *and* have respectively a participle and an adjective, then not Wærferth but the Reviser
repeats the auxiliary (106.1, 162.30 [the original translation
has two participles]). The Latin once has *sunt* in the first of two
phrases joined by *et* (137.26); otherwise no auxiliary.

b. Two other examples involve *sceol(d)on* and *het* governing
infinitives and *þæt*-clauses:

CO: he gegearwode and gecyðde us þæt (gecyðde[ ] **O**) in
þære bysene his w(e)orces to þon *þæt we sceol(d)on*
folgian (fyl[ ]n **O**) his swaðe be þam gemete ura (ussa
O) mæg(e)na and *þæt we sceoldon* (on) un-
forspurnedum fotum (unforspornenen fet **O**) þis(s)es
andweardan weorces (lifes **O**) gan on þone weg þæs
ec(e)an lifes (60.25)
H: þæt he gegearwode us on gebysnunge Godes weorces
to þam *þæt we* be gemete urra mægena *sceolon* fylian
his fotswaðe and unætspornenum fotum þyses andweardan weorkes gan on þone weg þæs ecean lifes
Ln: hoc nobis in exemplum actionis praebuit, *ut* pro
nostrarum uirium modulo eius uestigia sequentes, in-
offenso pede operis praesentis uitae carpamus uiam
(1.9.68)

CO: Benedictus . . . hine sylfne *het* (a)gan fram (from **O**)
þære þe(g)nunge and *het* þæt he of þære tide him
stille gesæte (ðære[ ] **O**) (144.19)
H: he . . . *het* hine gewitan fram þære þenunge and þæt
he of þære tide him stille sæte

Ln: ipsum uero *iussit* a ministerio recedere et sibi hora
  eadem quietum sedere (2.20.13)

Wærferth repeats the subject and, at 60.25, conjunction, as
well as the auxiliary (see §27.*b.* above).

Chapter 3

Word Order within Phrases or Clauses

§29. MOST OF THE REVISER'S CHANGES in word order bring the translation into accord with present-day English; a notable exception, his fondness for postpositions or verbal prefixes, which supersede Wærferth's prepositions (see §37.*b*.). Since the changes generally do not bring the translation into accord with the Latin, the Reviser makes them on the basis of his own language — his syntax or writing style. He joins modifiers to their heads, prepositions or postpositions to their objects. Modifiers exchange positions with one another and with their heads, usually giving the revision the word order that obtains today. The Reviser also places predicates after their verbs, as in present-day English. The adverb *þa*, vocatives, and interjections all assume new positions within the clause to sharpen the style.

Relative order of modifiers

§30. A possessive exchanges positions with an adjective (40.33, 110.13, 138.23), participle (78.10), number (96.4), or demonstrative pronoun 150.32),[1] e.g.,

> **CO**: þam *diglan Godes* dome (40.33)
> **H**: *Godes diglan* dome
> **Ln**: *occulto Dei* iudicio (1.4.226)

CO: mid (*def.* **O**) *his aþenedra (aðenedre* **O***)* handa (honda **O**) (78.10)

H: mid *aþenedre his* handa

Ln: extensa manu (1.10.103)

CO: *his seo (sio* **O***)* gemæne spræc (150.32)

H: *seo his* gemæne spræc

Ln: *ipsa* . . . communis *eius* locutio (2.23.1)

Since the preposition *mid* cannot take a genitive object,[2] at 78.10 manuscript **C**'s *aþenedra* either represents a scribal error for **aþenedre* or shows the loss of distinction between unaccented *-ra* and *-re*. The revision's phrase *mid aþenedre his handa* could operate as an absolute construction,[3] but compare the same version's prepositional phrase *of inneweardre his heortan*, with the word order attributive adjective, possessive pronoun (21.21; the original translation has *in his heortan ingehigdum [in-gehygdum* **O***]*, with the noun *ingehigdum* instead of the adjective *inneweardre*). Wærferth puts the possessive first in half of the examples, thereby agreeing with present-day English (78.10, 110.13, 150.32); in half the Reviser does so. When it has one, the Latin always puts its possessive after the adjective, number, or demonstrative (all but 78.10).

Modifier and head

§31. The Reviser joins, or at least brings closer together, modifiers and heads that lie separated in the original translation.[4] The modifiers include attributive adjectives, numbers, or pronouns (§32); attributive genitive or dative nouns or noun phrases (§33); names (§34); predicate participles or adjectives, including those in absolute constructions (§35); and adjective clauses (§36). He places the attributives before their heads, where they belong today, and the names and predicates after their heads, again as in present-day English.

§32. *a.* An adjective phrase or the pronoun *sylf*, with or without *him*, moves closer to its antecedent:

CO: *he* worhte sona *sylfa* þa mæg(e)n (20.3)
H: *he* sona *him sylf* geworhte þa mægenu
Ln: ipse fecit (1.2.85)

CO: hine þa manige (monige **O**) his *(ge)cuðra manna (monna*
O*)* geornlice acsodon (axodon **O**), *ge æþelcunde ge oðre*
(22.14)
H: þa beheoldon hine fela his *cuðra manna, ægðer ge*
æðelborene ge oðre
Ln: multi *uiri noti ac nobiles* . . . sollicite requirebant
(1.2.120)

On four other occasions nominative *(him) sylf(a)* (95.23,
110.20, 132.10) or accusative *sylfne* immediately follows its
head in the revision. Once, however, the first person pronoun
me sylf lies adjacent to its antecedent *ic* only in the original
translation (32.21), and once the Reviser shifts *ealle* from immediately before to a couple of words after its head (125.9, for
which see the next paragraph). Whenever the Latin has a corresponding construction, its word order agrees with that of the
revision (22.14, 32.21).

b. The number *twegen* (83.28) and the pronouns or adjectives
sum (23.30), *mænig* (43.27, the Reviser uses *sum*), *eall* (51.14,
67.9, 68.23, 76.12, 82.27 [five times]), and *sylf* (4.22, 28.5 [the
Reviser uses the adjective *swutol*], 156.29, 173.12) follow their
nouns or noun phrases in the original translation, precede in
the revision,[5] e.g.,

CO: þa wyrta ealle (67.9)
H: ealle þa wyrta
Ln: omne holus (1.9.169)

CO: þa locu seolf (sylf **O**) (4.22)
H: þa sylfan locu
Ln: ipsa . . . claustra (1.Prologue.21)

Elsewhere *eall* precedes a noun phrase in one version and follows the other version's corresponding demonstrative or personal pronoun: *ealle þa broþra* and *eallum þam oþrum (broðrum)* become *hi . . . ealle* (125.9) and *him eallum* (51.6) respectively, and *ealle þas þing* replaces *þas ealle* (138.8, def. **O**). Meanwhile the number *an* (30.8) and, used with *God*, the adjective *ælmihtig* (26.32, 33.25, 57.13, 85.35. 105.17 [five times]) come after a noun in the revision, e.g.,

> **CO**: his anum (anon **O**) worde (30.8)
> **H**: his worde anum
> **Ln**: solo uerbo (1.4.62)

> **CO**: ðæs ælmihtigan Godes (26.32)
> **H**: Godes ælmihtiges
> **Ln**: Dei omnipotentis (*v.l.* omnipotentis Dei) (1.4.15)

But Wærferth's phrase with *anum* probably means "his one word," the Reviser's, "his word alone"; and even present-day English allows the idiom "God almighty."[6] Of this paragraph's twenty-one examples, the Latin supports the revision in nine, the original translation in four (30.8, 85.35, 105.17, 138.8), neither version in seven (23.30, 28.5, 33.25, 51.6, 51.14, 125.9, 156.29), and at 26.32, both versions.

§33. *a.* The Reviser places an attributive genitive noun or noun phrase adjacent to its head, e.g.,

> **CO**: ne scealt þu hwæþre *þæs andgites* bedæled beon *þis(s)es*
> *eadigan mannes (monnes* **O**) *lifes Æquities* (33.13)
> **H**: swa þeah ne scealt þu beon bedæled *þære oncnawen-*
> *nysse þæs eadigan Æquities lifes*
> **Ln**: ne tamen *uitae eius cognitione* frauderis (1.4.106)

The single possible instance of the reverse phenomenon, with the noun phrase next to its head only in the original translation, may involve a genitive object rather than an attributive

(152.5). Parallel Latin words and phrases lie adjacent to each other nine times (33.13, 50.24, 52.20, 54.19, 72.5, 97.17, 117.22, 140.19, 152.5), apart three times (80.1, 101.12, 141.13 [om. **O**; Hecht emended manuscript **H**'s attributive pronoun *sumes* to *scipes*]). Once a dative attributive noun phrase separated from its head corresponds to a genitive:

> **CO**: þa wearð *his horse* asliden *se fot* (81.24)
>   **H**: þa wearð *his horses fot* asliden
> **Ln**: *equo (v.l. equi) eius pes* lapsus est (1.10.156)

In several analogous examples the attributives consist of pronouns or possessive adjectives, e.g., dative *us*, genitive or possessive *ure* (14.25, 20.9, 24.18 [om. **O**], 71.26, 79.16, 88.1, 157.7, 169.31 [eight times]: see §5 above, and compare 19.34, 22.10 [quoted in the next paragraph], and 36.29, with dative attributives in both versions). The Reviser once substitutes a prepositional phrase separated from its head for Wærferth's adjacent attributive genitive (77.23, quoted at the end of the next paragraph); and once when the revision has a genitive, the original translation has the appositive accusative *hors*:

> **CO**: hi þa *ealle heora (hiora* **O***) hors* æt (eft **O**) him to bryce
>   (brice **O**) and to nytnesse onfengon (onfe[ ]gon **O**)
>   (16.2)
>   **H**: þa underfengon hi *ealle* æt him *hyra horsa* to brucenne
>   and to notienne
> **Ln**: omnes a singulis reciperentur (1.2.35)

Compare the passages discussed in the previous two paragraphs.

b. On almost every page of the translation the Reviser moves all or part of an attributive genitive or (22.10, 36.29) dative noun or noun phrase, including names, from after its head to before,[7] e.g.,

CO: eallre þære gesomnunge (gesamnuncge **O**) þara
      broðra (29.6)
 H: þara broðra gesamnunge
Ln: fratrum congregatio (*v.l.* congregatio fratrum)
      (1.4.47)

CO: to lareowe þam abbude (22.10)
 H: þam abbode to lareowe
Ln: magistra . . . magistri (1.2.118)

Such passages outnumber their opposites, in which the Reviser
places the attributive after its head, by 110 to 18. The Latin
supports the revision slightly over half the time (fifty-eight
passages for which the attributive precedes its head in the revision, ten for which it follows), supports the original translation
over a third of the time (thirty-nine passages for which the attributive follows its head in the original translation, seven for
which it precedes), and supports neither or (29.6 quoted above
and 109.27) both versions about a ninth of the time (fourteen
passages).[8] In a few other instances the attributive, its head, or
both may consist of a pronoun (19.34, 79.26, 88.22, 89.5,
108.7, 140.10, 173.3 [seven times]),[9] e.g.,

CO: his wundra ænigu (ænegu **O**) (79.26)
 H: ænie his wundra
Ln: qua illius miracula (1.10.125)

CO: cwylmend (cwilme[ ] **O**) þæs mannes (monnes **O**)
      (89.5)
 H: his cwylmend
Ln: interfectorem illius (1.12.19)

In yet others a compound of the type noun plus noun replaces a
noun and its following genitive attributive (24.27, 118.13,
145.13, 163.27),[10] e.g.,

CO: þa tide his gereordnysse (gereordnesse **O**) (118.13)

H: his gereordungtide
Ln: horam . . . refectionis illius (2.8.23)

Finally, a genitive or dative noun phrase corresponds to a prepositional phrase (46.22, 77.23, 97.31 [quoted in §14.*c.* above]), e.g.,

> **CO**: þa helpe þæs halgan mannes þingunga (monnes
> geðingða **O**) (77.23)
> **H**: þurh his þingunga . . . help
> **Ln**: intercessionis eius opem (1.10.95)

The above paragraph also cites this particular passage.

§34. *a.* A name lies next to its correlative noun or noun phrase in the revision (29.30, 31.33, 43.30, 75.8, 116.27, 117.9 [om. **O**], 130.7, 140.5, 162.21 [nine times]) or original translation (127.30, 133.15, 154.27 [om. **C**]), e.g.,

> **CO**: *se Godes þeow* (cyrde), þeah he feor (fior **O**) wære,
> *Æquitius*, (þa he) hire hæle gecwæþ (29.30)
> **H**: *se Godes þeow Æquitius* hyre hæle gecwæð, þeah he
> feorr wære
> **Ln**: eandem salutem illius *Dei famulus Equitius* longe
> positus dixit (1.4.59)

> **CO**: þæs eadigan (eadegan **O**) *Stephanes* cyrice (cirice **O**)
> *þæs martyres (def.* **O**) (43.30)
> **H**: þæs eadigan *martires Stephanes* cyrce
> **Ln**: ecclesia beati *martyris Stephani (v.l., in Moricca, Stephani
> martyris)* (1.5.6)

The name and its noun or noun phrase constitute the subject of the clause (29.30 [see further §43 below], 75.8), a prepositional object (31.33), or an attributive genitive, divided in one version by the head word.[11] The Latin joins eleven of the pairs of names and referents, and omits the name in the twelfth passage (31.33).

b. The Reviser also shifts names from before to after their referent nouns or noun phrases,[12] and on one occasion he does the opposite:

> **CO:** þære cæstre (ceastre seo hatte **O**) Reatina (33.17)
> **H:** Reatine þære ceastre
> **Ln:** Reatinae (*v.l., in Moricca,* Reatinae urbis) (1.4.108)

Half the time the Latin has the word order of the original translation; half the time, that of the revision (33.17 [as v.l.], 43.30, 69.29, 130.19, 131.11 [five times]) or neither version (19.17, 33.17, 124.23).

§35. *a.* A predicate participle or adjective, along with any accompanying words, moves toward its predicated subject or object, e.g.,

> **CO:** *þa þearfan* ne eodon *æmtige* onweg fram (aweg from **O**) him (64.3)
> **H:** *þa þearfan idelhende* fram him ne eodon
> **Ln:** ne ab eo *pauperes uacui* exirent (1.9.120)

> **CO:** he . . . gesæde (asægde **O**) *þa wisan* him *swa gedone* (115.31)
> **H:** he . . . him rehte *þa þing swa gedon*
> **Ln:** *rem gestam* retulit (2.7.20)

The Reviser's predicate lies either next to the subject (64.3, 101.7, 105.33, 144.28, 149.15 [five times]) or object (115.31, 129.1, 130.5, 172.12), or merely closer (34.10, 97.27; both with predicated objects). On three other occasions a predicate moves away from the subject (101.19 [om. **C**], 124.13) or object (15.19). Wærferth on balance follows the Latin five times, and the Reviser does so five times (15.19, 34.10, 64.3, 97.27, 115.31); otherwise neither version corresponds to the Latin (101.7, 101.19, 144.28, 149.15). Compare the passages discussed in §36.*c.* below.

b. Predicate participles and adjectives also move from before to after their substantives, e.g.,

> **CO**: þa æt nehstan *mid þam witum oferswiðed se ceorl*
> geandette þæt he . . . (163.5)
> **H**: þa æt niextan *se ceorl mid þam witum oferswyðed*
> geandette þæt he . . .
> **Ln**: *uictus poenis rusticus* sese . . . professus est (2.31.9)

> **CO**: he . . . hire agæf (agef **O**) *þæt hriddern gesund* (97.26)
> **H**: he . . . hire ageaf *gehal þæt hridder*
> **Ln**: ei *sanum capisterium* reddidit (2.1.18)

The predicates belong to subjects (104.25, 124.13, 163.5) or objects (97.26, 172.12). Wærferth twice places the predicate first (124.13, 163.5); the Reviser does so three times. In a few instances the original translation's predicate participle or adjective following the subject (8.9 [om. **C**], 90.7) or object (17.15) corresponds to the revision's preceding attributive,[13] e.g.,

> **CO**: sum wi(i)f bær hire (hyre **O**) *sunu deadne* (17.15)
> **H**: sum wif bær hire *deadan sunu*
> **Ln**: quaedam mulier *extincti filii* corpusculum ferret
> (1.2.51)

In yet others predicate and head together form a dative absolute,[14] e.g.,

> **CO**: *þa gangendum (gongendum* **O***) þam broðrum þyder (ðider*
> **O***)*, Benedictus heom (him **O**) gehet . . . (147.26)
> **H**: *ðam broðrum þa utgangendum*, Benedictus behet . . .
> **Ln**: *quibus euntibus* spondit . . . (2.22.6)

So 51.6, 115.13, 133.1 (om. **C**; quoted in §50, note 16, below), and 147.20, for each of which Wærferth places the predicate first. Of this paragraph's thirteen examples, the Latin supports the Reviser's word order in seven, Wærferth's in four (90.7,

124.13, 163.5, 172.12), and in two the word order of neither writer (8.9, 115.13).

§36. *a.* The Reviser, often despite the Latin, pushes dozens of adjective clauses and their antecedents next to each other or (7.21, 63.16, 80.3) closer together,[15] e.g.,

> **CO:** *þæt leoht* wæs beorhtre þonne dæges leoht, *þæt þær lym(b)de betwyh þam þeostrum (þystrum* **O***)* (171.5)
>
> **H:** *þæt leoht þe þær lymde betweoh þam þystrum* wæs beorhtre þonne dæges leoht
>
> **Ln:** diem uinceret *lux illa, quae inter tenebras radiasset* (2.35.21)

In several of the passages one or both versions may repeat the antecedent, e.g.,

> **CO:** ic mihte (meahte **O**) *þa domas* witan and bodian, *þa þe* ic þe ongæt sæcgan (ongeat secgan **O**) (139.12)
>
> **H:** ic mihte witan and bodian *þa domas þe* ic oncneow þe sylfne secgean
>
> **Ln:** illa ego *iudicia* et nosse et pronuntiasse potui, *quae* te dixisse cognoui (2.16.72)

Wærferth's second *þa* represents either an antecedent or part of the adjective clause. Elsewhere manuscript **C** of the original translation (6.7), manuscript **O** (107.19, *þætte* for **þæt þe*), both **C** and **O** (15.31, 25.25, 33.18, 43.9), or all three manuscripts, including **H** of the revision (63.16, quoted by Timmer, *Studies*, p. 24), have such a pronoun before the relative particle *þe*. At 59.12, however, **C** has a relative phrase of the *se' þe* variety.[16] Of six contrary instances, where the Reviser has cut adjective clause and antecedent asunder, usually only the adverb *þa* (46.1, 80.23, 125.1) or the verb *is* (173.19) intervenes.[17]

b. Some adjective clauses are attended by following heads, e.g.,

CO: *þa þe þu sylfa ne spræce*, butan tweon on urum
ongytenessum (tweon ussum ongitenessum **O**) þu
behyd(d)est *þa* (139.14)

H: *þa þe þu sylf ne sprycst*, untwywlice *þa* þu behydst urum
oncnawennyssum

Ln: *ea, quae ipse non loqueris*, nostris procul dubio cogni-
tionibus abscondis (2.16.73)

The Reviser places the referent pronoun nearer, usually adjacent to its preceding clause. Either the Latin agrees with the
revision (60.21, 169.20), or its adjective clause does not have a
following referent (8.27 [def. **O**], 25.15 [quoted in §3 above],
25.21, 139.5, 139.14 [five times]).

c. Finally in a third set of examples a predicate phrase
supersedes Wærferth's adjective clause (see §48 below), e.g.,

CO: *sum man (mon* **O***)* wære in þære ylcan (ilcan **O**)
mægðe *þam wæs nama Matirius (noma Martyrius* **O***)*
(86.25)

H: on þære ylcan mægðe wæs *sum man Martirius genemned*

Ln: *quidam* namque in eadem prouincia, *Martyrius nomine,*
. . . fuit (1.11.1)

The predicate immediately follows its referent, the adjective
clause does not (compare the material discussed in §35.*a.*
above). The Latin parallels Wærferth's word order twice
(70.34, 86.25) and the Reviser's once (162.18).

Preposition or postposition and object

§37. *a.* Prepositions and postpositions lie closer to their objects
in one version than in the other. Whenever both versions have
a postposition, it lies closer to its object in the revision (36.1,
58.30, 66.5), e.g.,

CO: hi(e) *him* cwædon *to* (36.1)
H: hi cwædon *him to*
Ln: qui dixerunt (1.4.147)

More commonly, either or both particles may represent verbal prefixes rather than postpositions,[18] e.g.,

CO: *heom (him* **O***)* wæs þus *to* sprecende and cwæð
    (105.15)
H: *him* þus *to* spræc
Ln: *ad*locutus est (*v.l.,* in *Moricca,* est *eos*), dicens (2.3.32)

On other occasions Wærferth's or (37.8) the Reviser's preposition adjacent to its object corresponds to the other writer's postposition or verbal prefix separated from the object (7.6, 24.5 [quoted in note 20 of the next paragraph], 37.8, 59.14 [om. **C**], 81.17, 89.31, 144.7 [seven times]). For about half of this paragraph's examples the Latin also has a particle and object, either adjoining (59.14, 66.5, 73.31, 79.13, 81.17, 89.31, 124.33, 138.33 [as v.l.] [eight times]) or apart (36.16, 78.3, 105.15 [as v.l.], 138.33, 144.7 [five times]).

b. The Reviser often substitutes postpositions or verbal prefixes for Wærferth's prepositions,[19] e.g.,

CO: he his feorh aþrang (oðþrang **O**) *of þam lichaman*
    (*lichoman* **O**) (136.2)
H: he his sawle *him fram* asceoc
Ln: animam eius excuteret (2.16.21)

Fram may either represent a postposition or form part of the verb: Clark Hall-Meritt recognizes *framascæcan,* "to shake off," but Bosworth-Toller-Campbell does not. The Reviser twice uses a preposition instead of Wærferth's postposition or verbal prefix (37.8, 135.26 [om. **C**; quoted in §14 above]); twice he uses the preposition *ætforan* instead of the divided form found in the original translation, with the object between *æt* and *foran* (20.28, 143.33 [om. **C**]). The two versions have different particles in some of the examples — the original translation's *for* versus the revision's *fore* (38.1), *wið/ongean* (40.2), *in/on* (59.14, 141.15: see §13.*a.* above), *be* or *bi/ymbe* (81.17), *ofer/toforan* (135.26), *of/fram* (136.2), *beforan/æt* (144.7); different kinds of objects in some — the original translation's noun phrase or form of the demonstrative *se* versus the revision's personal pronoun (80.15, 82.16, 127.8, 132.15, 136.2, 149.4, 170.2 [seven times]),[20] demonstrative *se* or personal pronoun/pronominal adverb *þær* (21.34, 40.2, 116.1, 141.15, 142.5 [five times]), demonstrative *se* used as a relative/indeclinable relative pronoun *þe* (59.14, 81.17). Twice the preposition takes an accusative object and the postposition a dative (38.1 and 156.11, cited or quoted in §13.*d.* and *b.* respectively). For about two-fifths of the passages the Latin has a particle that may serve as a preposition (20.28, 28.10, 38.1, 59.14, 80.13, 81.17, 125.18, 132.2, 143.33, 156.11, 170.2 [eleven times]) or postposition (80.15, 89.31, 128.10, 135.26, 144.7 [five times]).

Predicate participle or adjective and auxiliary

§38. The predicate participle or adjective, usually of a subordinate clause, reverses positions with its auxiliary, a form of *beon/wesan*, *weorþan*, or *habban*, e.g.,

CO: þa earcan (earce **O**) þe *(a)seted wæs* ofer þa byrgen(n)e (42.7)
H: þa earce þe *wæs asett* ofer his byrgenne
Ln: arcam, quae super*posita* sepulcro eius *fuerat* (1.4.243)

CO: þæt hit *riht nære* (68.18)
H: þæt hit *nære riht*
Ln: quod *iustum non esset* (1.9.185)

Wærferth's participle or adjective precedes the auxiliary, the Reviser's follows, thirty-seven of forty-one times.[21] Most of the examples involve past participles, but seven involve adjectives (5.32, 45.2, 62.28, 63.17, 68.18, 89.13, 148.3) and one a present participle.[22] In two others *gewis(s)* and/or *cuð* may represent either an adjective or a past participle (3.9, 55.27).[23] Both versions of the translation have a form of the auxiliary *weorþan* at 16.29, 22.24, and 30.26; at 76.18 the revision has *wearð*, the original translation *wæs*. The single example with a form of *habban* depends on restoring manuscript **O**'s lost text:

> **C**: hire hwæte . . . , eall þæt heo ofer gær habban
> scolde to bygleofan (68.26)
> **O**: hire hwæte . . . , þone þe hio ær hire sylfre to ealles
> geares andlyfne *g[e]g[earwod hæfde]*
> **H**: eallne þone hwæte þe heo *hæfde* hire *begiten* to ealles
> geares andlyfene
> **Ln**: omne triticum, quod sibi in stipendio totius anni
> parauerat (1.9.188)

Though here only the two yoghs (printed *g*) survive of *gegearwod hæfde*,[24] the variation *gegearwi(ge)an* **CO**, *begitan* **H** has remained intact at 19.33. The Latin uses a corresponding construction with participle or adjective plus form of *sum* for about half of the passages: the Latin participles and adjectives normally precede,[25] occasionally follow their auxiliaries (5.32, 7.17, 46.23, 148.3).

Predicate substantive or infinitive and verb

§39. The verb *beon/wesan* of a subordinate or (172.21) independent clause trades positions also with a predicate noun phrase, number, or infinitive,[26] e.g.,

> **CO**: efne swa swa hit *sum(es) deaþes plyht (plih[ ]* **O**) *oððe
> scyfe wære* (15.9)
> **H**: swilce hit *wære sum deaðes scyfe*
> **Ln**: quasi mortale praecipitium (1.2.22)

The Reviser's noun phrase follows the verb here and at four other places (50.32, 74.8, 131.16, 172.21); Wærferth's does so at 89.5 and 136.17 (om. **O**). Three passages involve the number *an* or an infinitive, e.g.,

> **CO**: swa swiðe swa hi *an beoð* mid Driht(e)ne (138.15)
> **H**: swa swyðe swa hi *beoð an* samod mid Drihtne
> **Ln**: in quantum cum Domino sunt (*v.l., in Moricca, unum sunt*) (2.16.58)

> **CO**: cwys(t) þu hwæþer hit *to (ge)lyfenne sy (si* **O**) þæt þysum (þisum **O**) Godes ðeowan mihte (þeowe meahte **O**) symble æt beon se witedomes gast (146.2)
> **H**: cwyst þu hwæðer hit *sy to gelyfenne* þæt þysum Godes þeowe mihte symle æt beon þære witegunge gast
> **Ln**: dic . . . numquidnam *credendum est* huic Dei famulo semper prophetiae spiritum adesse potuisse (2.21.17)

At 3.15, though, *ana* moves from after to before *bið*. The Latin has Wærferth's word order three times (131.16, 138.15 [as v.l.], 146.2), the Reviser's once (136.17).

Position of the adverb *þa*

§40. The Reviser takes extraordinary care with the adverb *þa*. If a subordinate clause precedes, he positions *þa* at the beginning of the main clause to make clear the temporal correlation of the two clauses, e.g.,

> **CO**: þa þam Godes mæn (menn **O**) his a(ge)n hors gegifen (agifen **O**) wæs, hi *þa* ealle heora (hiora **O**) hors æt (eft **O**) him to bryce (brice **O**) and to nytnesse onfengon (onfe[ ]gon **O**) (15.35)
> **H**: þa þam Godes þeowe wæs his an hors agifen, *þa* underfengon hi ealle æt him hyra horsa to brucenne and to notienne
> **Ln**: dum seruo Dei unus suus caballus redditur, omnes a singulis reciperentur (1.2.34)

Other subordinate clauses begin with the temporal conjunctions *þa þa* (22.11 [*þa* **O**], 24.20, 26.21 [the original translation has an independent rather than a subordinate clause], 88.21, 104.30, 127.14 [*ða* **O**; for the main clause, the original translation has the adverb *sona* instead of *þa*] [six times]) and *sona swa* (50.17, om. **O**).[27] If, however, a subordinate clause does not precede, the Reviser moves *þa* away from the beginning, e.g.,

> **CO**: *þa* gecyrde (oncirde **O**) he hine to þam ilcum (ilcan **O**) emelum (67.10)
> **H**: and he *þa* bewende hine to þam ylcan emelum
> **Ln**: ad easdem erucas conuersus (1.9.169)

The adverb *þa* comes first in the original translation, or immediately follows a coordinating conjunction *and* or (141.5) *ac*, sixty-four of sixty-six times.[28] In nine additional examples the interjection *hwæt* or another adverb or two precedes *þa*, e.g.,

> **CO**: witodlice *þa* com se man(n) to þam mynstre (157.28)
> **H**: witodlice he becom *þa* to mynstre
> **Ln**: uenit itaque ad monasterium (2.27.5)

Wærferth's *þa* immediately follows *and eac* (145.8), *soðlice* (82.19), *swa na* (151.28), *and þær* (101.18), and *witodlice* (134.33, 157.28); the Reviser's *þa* immediately follows *hwæt* (21.22, 36.26, 169.10). Of this paragraph's eighty-three examples, the Latin has a word that may correspond to *þa* in twenty-two. The corresponding Latin word fifteen times begins the clause, comes later seven times.[29]

Position of a vocative or interjection

§41. The Reviser moves vocatives and interjections forward, e.g.,

> **CO**: geseoh (beseah **O**) þu, *sunu*, be þære flascan (flaxan **O**) (142.2)
> **H**: *sunu*, foresceawa be þære flaxan

Ln: uide, *fili*, de illo flascone (2.18.8)

CO: for hwon, *la*, wolde (woldon **O**) ge wiþ me þus
    (ge)don (105.17)
 H: *la*, for hwi woldon ge þus don wið me
Ln: quare in me facere ista uoluistis (2.3.33)

The third person vocative corresponds to the clause's second
person subject, sometimes unexpressed (38.19, 142.2, 172.32).
Wærferth places the interjection *la* within the clause, the
Reviser places it before (7.30, 105.17). The Latin sustains
Wærferth's placement of the vocatives but does not have any
interjections.

Chapter 4

The Use of Phrases and Clauses

§42. MANY OF THE CHANGES made by the Reviser affect the
order, type, or number of clauses in the translation. The last
chapter found him moving adjective clauses closer to their head
words (§36); the Reviser also moves adverb clauses from the
beginning or middle of their head clauses to the end (§43). He
replaces Wærferth's independent clauses with adverb or adjective clauses (§44), and replaces both independent and dependent clauses either with participles or participial phrases, including absolutes (§§46-50), or with infinitives or infinitive
phrases (§§51-52).

Position of an adverb clause

§43. The adverb clause follows its head clause in the revision,
e.g.,

> CO: forþon we magon witan þæt *þonne se gast wile*, he
> geeðað (146.13)
> H: swa is eac to witenne þæt he orðað *þonne he wyle*
> Ln: ita sciendum est quia et *quando uult* adspirat (2.21.24)

> CO: eac se ylca (ilca **O**) Paulus, to þan (to to þon **O**) *þæt*
> *he gecyðde hine sylfne (selfne **O**) cunnan hwylce wæren*
> *(wæron **O**) Godes gestihtunge*, he þas word (to) geecte
> (geihte **O**) (137.6)

H: eac se ylca Paulus þær to geihte *þæt he ætywde hine*
       sylfne cunnan þa þing þe syndon Godes gestihtunge
Ln: qui, *ut se ostenderet nosse quae Dei sunt*, adiunxit
        (2.16.38)

Wærferth's adverb clause either precedes the head clause, as at
146.13, or lies within it, as at 137.6.[1] The Reviser once moves
an adverb clause, governed by *þeah þe*, from within to before its
head clause (4.20). At 146.13 both the head clause and the
adverb clause follow a governing conjunction *þæt*; so the
passages at 57.27, 106.10, and 158.28. On another occasion
manuscript **C** of the original translation repeats *þæt* at the
beginning of each clause (see §27.*a.* above):

CO: se arwyrða (arwurða **O**) wer . . . bebead þam
        mæssepreoste *þæt* swa lange (longe **O**) swa he sylfa
        leofode on lichaman (selfa lyfde in lichoman **O**), *þæt*
        *(om. **O**)* he næfre ænigum (ænegum **O**) men (ne)
        sæde (asægde **O**) þis wundor (59.22)
 H: se bisceop . . . bebead þam mæssepreoste *þæt* he
        nanum men þis wundor ne asæde swa lange swa he
        sylf on lichaman lifde
 Ln: presbitero praecepit, ne, quousque ipse in corpore
        uiueret, hoc miraculum cuilibet indicaret (1.9.50)

And on three occasions *þæt* only follows, does not precede,
Wærferth's adverb clause (61.33, 139.31, 148.26), e.g.,

CO: ac ic þe bidde, *gif hwylce syn (sin **O**) nu gyt (git **O**) to*
        *sæcganne be þam mæg(e)ne þyses (þises **O**) halgan weres*
        Benedictes, þæt þu (þa) gecyðe (139.31)
 H: ac ic bidde þe *þæt* þu gita gerecce *gif þu hwilce ma wite*
        be þyses weres Benedictes mægene
 Ln: sed quaeso te, *si qua sunt adhuc de huius uiri uirtute*,
        subiunge (2.16.81)

Since the Latin supports the Reviser only when he puts the
adverb clause first (4.20), and otherwise parallels the original

translation: when the Reviser does the opposite — puts the head clause first — presumably he either follows the norm of his language or dialect, or tries to make a special impression.[2]

Independent or dependent clause

§44. Wærferth's pair of mutually independent clauses corresponds to an adverb or adjective clause plus a main clause, e.g.,

> **CO**: and *he þa se seoca mann (monn* **O**) *eft acwicod (acwicad* **O**) *dyde dædbote seofon dagas for his þam ær gefremedum synnum*; and þy eahtoðan dæge he geferde (gewat **O**) bliðe of þam lichaman (lichoman **O**) (90.7)
> **H**: and *þa þa se edcukeda seoca seofon dagas dyde dædbote and behreosunge for his ær gefremodum gyltum,* þa on þam eahteoðan dæge ferde he bliðe of þam lichaman
> **Ln**: et *dum per dies septem de perpetratis culpis paenitentiam aeger rediuiuus ageret,* octauo die laetus de corpore exiuit (1.12.36)

> **CO**: and *hi na (no* **O**) *ne scrifan þeh hi eallinga (scrifon þeah[ ]lenga* **O**) *hire sawle adwæsctan (saule adwæscton* **O**); *þa ongunnon hi helpan hire lichaman (hi[ ]lichoman* **O**) *mid heora (hiora* **O**) *drycræftum to sumre hwile* (73.20)
> **H**: and *ne hogodon na þeah hi eallunga hyre sawle adwæscton, þa þe woldon mid drycræftum hyre lichaman to sumre hwile gehelpan*
> **Ln**: ut eius animam funditus extinguerent, *cuius carni magicis artibus ad tempus prodesse conarentur* (1.10.38)

The temporal conjunction *þa þa* governs all thirteen of the Reviser's adverb clauses, twelve of which precede their head clauses (all but that at 69.10, where Hecht punctuated the revision for an independent rather than an adverb clause); both adjective clauses begin with the indeclinable relative pronoun *þe*.[3]

In two other instances Wærferth has the adverb clause, governed by *þa þa* (124.19, *ða þe* **O**) or *sona swa* (46.10). The independent clauses either lie in apposition or (31.3, 69.10, 90.7, 140.8, 140.32 [five times]) are joined by *and*. By subordinating Wærferth's clauses in these ways, with temporal conjunctions and with relatives, the Reviser both conforms to the Latin and achieves greater coherence. Robinson has neatly summarized the different ways of translating: "It has been observed that when an Old English translator is confronted by a complicated Latin sentence with interlocking clauses he will often take the easy way of breaking the thought down into two or more simple Old English sentences, even though the vernacular is known to have been capable of hypotactic as well as paratactic constructions."[4]

Clause or phrase

§45. Important advances in conciseness, as well as conformity with the Latin, come from the Reviser's decision to combine clauses. A participle or participial phrase supersedes Wærferth's independent, adverb, or noun clause (§§46–47); an adjective, adjective phrase, participle, or participial phrase supersedes his adjective clause (§48). Absolute constructions likewise replace Wærferth's independent, adverb, or noun clauses (§§49–50),[5] and infinitives or infinitive phrases replace noun or adverb *þæt*-clauses (§§51–52).

§46. Twenty of Wærferth's independent clauses correspond to predicate participles or participal phrases,[6] e.g.,

> **CO**: þa sona eft se halga man (monn **O**) ageaf (eft) þam
> Gotan þone geloman (þæt bill **O**) *and þus cwæð to him*
> (114.17)
>
> **H**: he þa hrædlice ageaf þam Gotan þæt tol *þus cweðende*
> **Ln**: qui statim ferramentum Gotho reddidit, *dicens*
> (2.6.20)

On five other occasions the original translation has the participial phrase (25.18, 32.19, 68.17, 85.5, 85.14). Each of the twenty-five examples involves a present participle (but compare that quoted at the end of this paragraph), and the Latin has a matching participle or participial phrase for all but one (78.23). Most of the passages resemble that just quoted: clause plus clause corresponds to clause plus participle or participial phrase, in that order.[7] Five of them, however, show another arrangement (24.4 [quoted in §37.*b.*, note 20, above], 62.16, 103.30, 135.27, 154.12), e.g.,

> **CO**: þa þa sum Benedictes cniht ([ ]cniht **O**) se wæs
> munuc lufode his magas ofer þæt þe he mid rihte
> sceolde (of[ ] **O**), *and geneahhe higode* and ferde to
> heora (hiora **O**) huse . . . (154.12)
>
> **H**: þa þa sum Benedictes munuccnapana lufode his
> magas ofer þæt þe he sceolde, and to hyra huse for
> *yrnende . . .*
>
> **Ln**: dum quidam eius puerulus monachus, parentes suos
> ultra quam debebat diligens atque ad eorum
> habitaculum *tendens* . . . (2.24.3)

The Reviser's participle *yrnende* supersedes Wærferth's first clause, *and geneahhe higode.*[8] Even though governed ultimately by a subordinating conjunction *þa þa*, the clause in question stands independent of a second clause, *and ferde to heora huse*, with which the Reviser merges it. Both independent clauses always have the same subject, whether expressed or not; the conjunction *and* usually joins them,[9] though sometimes not, e.g.,

> **CO**: symle (sym[ ]le **O**) he sceawode beforan þam eagum
> his scyppendes; *symble (sym[ ]le **O**) he wæs smeagende
> (ymbe) hine sylfne (selfne **O**)* (107.14)
>
> **H**: he simle hine sylfne besceawode beforan his scyppendes eagum *hine sylfe symle ameriende*
>
> **Ln**: ante oculos conditoris se semper aspiciens, *se semper
> examinans* (2.3.62)

At 68.17 the Reviser dispenses with a coordinating conjunction, and at 32.19 he repeats the subject. On two other occasions the expected auxiliary *wæs* fails to appear in the second clause:

> **CO:** he . . . þa þone forðfarenan (forðferdan **O**) be naman (noman **O**) (ge)cigde mid unhlud(d)re stefne *þus cweþende*:"Waca broðor Marcelle" (85.5)
>
> **H:** he . . . mid unludre stefne þone forðfarenan be his naman nemde and clypode *and þus cweðende*: "Waca broðor Marcelle"
>
> **Ln:** non autem grandi uoce defunctum per nomen uocauit, *dicens*: "Frater Marcelle" (1.10.209)

> **CO:** he (*def.* **O**) wæs standende æt þam ehþyrle (mynstre **O**) *and gebiddende him to þam ælmihtigan (ælmih[ ]gan **O**) Drihtne* (170.32)
>
> **H:** þa gestod he þurhwacol æt anum eahþyrle *biddende þone ælmihtigan Drihten*
>
> **Ln:** ad fenestram stans et *omnipotentem Dominum deprecans* (2.35.18)

For the Reviser's *and þus cweðende*, understand *and þus cweðende wæs*;[10] for Wærferth's *and gebiddende*, understand *and wæs gebiddende* (compare the sentences discussed in §28.*a.* above). At three other places only manuscript **O** leaves *wæs* unexpressed (32.26, 62.16, 85.14). Supplying the original translation with a second clause, *(and) cwæð*, creates a twenty-sixth example:

> **CO:** he wære to him sylfum (selfum **O**) gecyr(r)ed [(and) cwæð]: "Nu ic wat . . . " (107.22)
>
> **H:** he þa to him sylfum gecyrred cwæð: "Nu ic wat . . . "
>
> **Ln:** ad se reuersus, dixit: "Nunc scio . . . " (2.3.66)

The Reviser's predicate participle *gecyrred* supersedes Wærferth's verbal phrase *wære gecyr(r)ed*.

§47. Predicate participles also replace adverb or noun clauses, e.g.,

> **CO**: and *þa þa se Godes wer gehyrde þa(s) word be þam nun-num*, he onbead sona to heom (him **O**) (152.7)
>
> **H**: se Godes wer *þa þas word gehyrende* him sona bebead
>
> **Ln**: uir autem Dei *haec de illis audiens*, eis protinus mandauit (2.23.21)

The original translation usually has a temporal adverb clause governed by *þa (þa)* (30.18, 42.31, 86.8, 114.10, 152.7, 173.21 [six times]) or *sona swa* (30.9, 97.20, 149.16). But *swa (swa)* or *swilce* twice governs an adverb clause of manner[11] —

> **CO**: and swa hit wæs to ongitanne (ongytanne **O**) þæt (and **O**) swa swa . . . þæt win nære na elles geeced (geiced **O**) ac *swylce hit þær in(ne) we(a)xende wære* (66.26)
>
> **H**: swilce þæt win nære na geiced ac wære akenned *weaxende*
>
> **Ln**: ac si . . . , uinum non augeretur, sed nasceretur (1.9.164)

—and on two occasions Wærferth's noun clause disappears, replaced by a participial phrase:

> **CO**: hi geleornodon (geleornedon **O**) *þæt hi sæ(g)don Drihtne þancas (þoncas **O**)* (145.31)
>
> **H**: hi þa *Drihtne þanciende* eallunga ongeaton
>
> **Ln**: *Domino gratias referentes*, didicerunt iam (2.21.15)

—and on two occasions Wærferth's noun clause disappears, replaced by a participial phrase:

> **CO**: hi geleornodon (geleornedon **O**) *þæt hi sæ(g)don Drihtne þancas (þoncas **O**)* (145.31)
>
> **H**: hi þa *Drihtne þanciende* eallunga ongeaton
>
> **Ln**: *Domino gratias referentes*, didicerunt iam (2.21.15)

CO: hwæt his leomu sceolan wilnian (limu sceolon willan
    O) þæt we wæron oððe hwæt *hi sceolan nyllan (sceolon
    nellan* **O**) (61.17)
  H: hwæt his limu scylon gewilnian oððe hwæt eac be *him
    nellendum* gewurðan sceoldon
  Ln: quid uelle eius membra debeant quidue de *eis* etiam
    nolentibus fiat (1.9.78)

The Reviser himself once uses a noun clause to clarify an
awkward passage:

CO: se ylca (ilca **O**) þeg(e)n, *þæt his hors þe* he geseah *acyr-
    red (acirred* **O**) fram (from **O**) his wedendra heorta
    (wedenheortnesse **O**) . . . (78.15)
  H: se ilca þegen geseah *þæt his hors wæs awended* fram his
    wodnysse . . .
  Ln: isdem milis *equum suum, quem* . . . a sua uesania uidit
    inmutatum (1.10.107)

The full context, quoted above in §40, note 27, suggests
Wærferth's *þæt* represents a demonstrative pronoun modifying
hors. Ten of the fourteen examples involve present participles;
four, past participles (30.18, 42.31, 78.15, 173.21). Except for
the passage at 66.26, the Latin always has a participle or participial phrase.

§48. An adjective clause corresponds to a predicate participial
phrase (69.28, 71.1, 86.26 [quoted in §36.*c.* above], 140.3,
162.18 [five times]), an attributive participle (56.1, 71.9,
124.29, 131.25), or an adjective or participle used as a noun
(23.1, 68.19, 97.34, 98.1). The original translation has ten of
the adjective clauses, the revision three (56.1, 97.34, 98.1).
The Latin never has a corresponding clause. Of the five
predicate phrases, four comprise a name followed by the past
participle *genemned*, supplanting Wærferth's relative clauses of
þam wæs nama followed by the name. The fifth phrase contains a
present participle:

CO: an fox *se c(w)om geneah(c)he naht feorran (noht feo[ ]ran*
   O) (69.28)
 H: an fox *cumende of þam neahlande*
Ln: *ex uicinitate* uulpes *ueniens* (1.9.203)

All four attributive participles precede their heads and decline weak. If, as in the passage just quoted involving a predicate participle, the antecedent serves as subject of the adjective clause, then the other version's attributive has the present tense (124.29, 131.25). If the antecedent serves as a (direct) object, then the other version has a past (passive) attributive participle, e.g.,

CO: of þam mannum *þe hi ær geswencton* (71.9)
 H: of þam *asettum* mannum
Ln: ab *obsessis* corporibus (1.10.4)

Both Wærferth and the Reviser use adjectives or (present) participles as nouns, e.g.,[12]

CO: þa *andweardan* ealle and eac þa *æfterfylgendan (æfter-*
   fylgendum **O)** ongætan (ongean **O)** (97.34–98.1)
 H: ægðer ge þa þe þær þa andwearde wæron ge þa þe þær
   syððon æfterfyligdon ealle oncneowon
Ln: et *praesentes* et *secuturi* omnes agnoscerent (2.1.22)

Elsewhere the revision's nouns *efenlæcendras* and *wædla* correspond to whole adjective clauses that include the words *onhergend* (23.1) and *wædla* (68.19).

§49. The Reviser substitutes absolute constructions, as well as predicate participles (see §46 above), for Wærferth's independent clauses, e.g.,

CO: and þa semnin(c)ga on þa tid þære stillan nihte
   (neahte **O)** *he wæs forð lociende* and geseah ufan
   onsended leoht (170.33)

H: and þa færinga on þam timan þære nihte stillnysse
   him ut lociendum, geseah he ufan onsended leoht
Ln: subito intempesta noctis hora *respiciens*, uidit fusam
   lucem desuper (2.35.19)

The absolute's present participle *lociendum* indicates an ongoing
action. Both versions of the translation have only one subject,
he or, within the revision's absolute construction, *him*. For the
other examples with present participles, each version has two
subjects: 114.30 quoted below, and

CO: *þa oðre broðra (broþru* **O***) hi reston*; he wæs (rest[ ]
   O) standende æt þam ehþyrle (mynstre **O**) (170.30)
H: *þam broðrum restendum*, þa gestod he . . . æt anum
   eahþyrle
Ln: adhuc *quiescentibus fratribus*, . . . ad fenestram stans
   (2.35.16)

The subject *he* of Wærferth's second clause remains the subject
of the revision's single clause; Wærferth's first subject *þa broðra*
becomes the dative "subject" of the absolute expression *þam
broðrum restendum*. Five remaining examples involve past participles: a direct object found in Wærferth's first clause becomes
the dative subject of the Reviser's absolute (88.11, 89.17,
125.27, 133.3, 148.4), e.g.,

CO: and *þa sænde (sende* **O***) he þa broðra (broþro* **O***) ut* and
   beleac þa cytan (125.27)
H: and *ut asendum þam broðrum*, he beleac þa cytan
Ln: *missis*que foras *fratribus* cellam clausit (2.11.20)

The direct object *þa broðra* turns up as "subject" of the phrase *ut
asendum þam broðrum*. The absolute comes at the beginning of its
clause four times, at the end once:

CO: *hi sendon forð swiþe wundorlicu (sen[ ]wundorlice* **O***) stefne*
   and ongunnon wepan for þam (*def.* **O**) gefean (89.17)

H: hi for þære blisse ongunnon swyðor wepan, *forð asen-dum stefnum micelre wundrunge*

Ln: *admirationis uocibus emissis*, coeperunt amplius prae gaudio flere (1.12.25)

Of all eight absolutes, seven have the dative case, one the nominative:[13]

C: and *sylf æfter gefeoll*; þa underfeng hine sona seo yþ (114.30)

O: and eac swylce *he s[ ]wæter gefeoll*; þa underfeng sona[ ]

H: and eac *he sylf feallende him æfter fyliende*, hine þa sona seo yð gegrap

Ln: *ipse* quoque *cadendo secutus est*. Quem mox unda rapuit (2.7.4)

As the passage stands in manuscript **H**, the Reviser's *he* has no verb, only the participles *feallende* and *fyliende* with which it can form an absolute phrase. Hecht created a clause, though, by adding *wæs* after *feallende*. The Latin has two clauses here and at 133.3 (as v.l., in Moricca); elsewhere, either an ablative absolute or (170.33) a nominative predicate participle. *And* usually joins Wærferth's clauses but fails to do so both here and at 170.30 (def.**O**).

§50. The Latin has an absolute construction for all five of the passages in which one version's absolute corresponds to the other's adverb or noun clause. Both of the passages with present absolute participles involve two subjects, e.g., *se Godes wer* (or *þeow*) and *hi/him*:

CO: *þa se ylca* (ilca **O**) *Godes wer þær æt wæs and hi þær betweonan heom* (him betweonan **O**) *spræcon*, þa ongæt (ongeat **O**) se Godes wer (þeow **O**) . . . (87.6)

H: þa wæs þær mid se ilca Godes þeow, and *him þa him betweonan sprecendum*, he oncneow . . .

Ln: isdem Dei famulus adfuit, *eis*que *referentibus*, . . .
   cognouit (1.11.8)

Wærferth uses the other present participle:

   C: *þam habbude þa gyt feorr gangende*, se cniht sæde . . .
      (37.14)
   O: *þone abbud ða git feor gongende*, se cniht sægde . . .
   H: *ða þa he þa gita wæs feorron þyderweard*, þa sæde se
      cniht . . .
   Ln: *quem adhuc longe positum (v.l., in Moricca, posito)* puer
      . . . indicauit (1.4.172)

Manuscript **O**'s *þone abbud . . . gongende* represents either a
calque on Latin *quem . . . posito* or a purely accusative absolute
with *gongende* reduced from **gongendne*.[14] **C**'s *þam habbude . . .
gangende* may represent either a conscious mixture of dative and
instrumental forms or the imperfect conversion of an accusative into a dative absolute.[15] The remaining three examples all contain absolute phrases with dative past participles.
In one the direct object of the adverb clause in the original
translation, becomes the passive "subject" of the participle in
the revision:[16]

   CO: *þa þa he his gebedu gedon hæfde*, he . . . untynde (on-
      tynde **O**) þæt winern (59.8)
   H: *geendodum his gebede*, he geopenode þæt winern
   Ln: *oratione facta*, apothecam aperuit (1.9.45)

To get the same pattern in another of the examples transform
Wærferth's passive into an active construction:

   CO: *þa þis þus gefylled wæs*, se ealda man (mon **O**) þa gyt
      tihhode (git tihade **O**) . . . (83.9)
   H: *witodlice þysum þus geendodum*, se ealda man
      geteohhode . . .
   Ln: *his igitur expletis*, studebat adhuc senex . . . (1.10.181)

Wærferth's *þa þis þus gefylled wæs* means **þa he þis þus gefylled hæfde*. The absolute phrases quoted so far correspond to temporal adverb clauses governed by *þa (þa)*. For one last passage, however, the Reviser's absolute allows him to dispense with a noun *þæt*-clause:

> **CO**: and hi þa *ongunnon þeahti(ge)an þæt hi* gemængdon (gemegndon **O**) attor wið wine (104.28)
> **H**: hi þa *ongunnenum geþeahte* gemengdon attor wið wine
> **Ln**: qui, *inito consilio*, uenenum uino miscuerunt (2.3.23)

Compare the last passage quoted in §21.*d.* above.

§51. An infinitive or infinitive phrase often replaces a *þæt*-clause,[17] e.g.,

> **CO**: genoh gerisenlice þu *hit* secest, *þæt þu wilt witan* (44.32)
> **H**: genoh gerisenlice þu secst *to witanne*
> **Ln**: congrue requiris (1.5.23)

Here Wærferth's object pronoun *hit* confirms the substantive nature of the following clause: *þæt þu wilt witan* serves as the direct object of *secest* (compare the sentences of §25.*b.* above). In five examples, however, *to þon* precedes the *þæt*-clause, either immediately (73.17, 97.2, 147.18) or one or two words earlier (71.6, 155.32), indicating the clause's adverbial nature,[18] e.g.,

> **CO**: he onsænde (onsende **O**) his þegnas to his tune *to þon þæt hi(e) sceoldon þær an mynster getrymman (getimbrian* **O***)* (147.18)
> **H**: he sceolde asendan his leorningcnihtas *mynster to timbrienne on his tune*
> **Ln**: missis discipulis suis, *construere monasterium debuisset* (2.22.3)

A few of the remaining thirty-seven examples may involve

adverb clauses, but most involve noun clauses. On three other occasions the Reviser not Wærferth uses a noun clause: 34.6 and 68.23 quoted below, and

> **CO**: nis hit na (no **O**) þæt, Petrus, þæt(te) Drihten wolde
> *aht (oht **O**) swylces beon* (61.13)
>   **H**: eornostlice Drihten nolde na *þæt æni þing swilces*
> *gewurde*
> **Ln**: non ergo Dominus uoluit *quicquam fieri* (1.9.76)

The revision's phrases usually contain or comprise *to* plus inflected infinitive — so the first two quoted above. An uninflected infinitive, without *to*, occurs nine times: at 77.8, 123.27, and 144.17 quoted below, as well as at 109.19, 125.16, 128.30, 131.33, 133.17, and 169.9. The verbs of the main clause and the *þæt*-clause invariably have the same tense and ordinarily may have the same mood. Three times, however, Wærferth's main clause has an indicative, his *þæt*-clause a subjunctive verb (30.6 quoted below, 76.25, 138.2 [def.**O**]).[19] Most of the *þæt*-clauses have either a simple verb or a modal auxiliary plus infinitive;[20] the four containing resolved tenses with *beon/wesan* or *habban* plus past participle receive further treatment below (34.6, 55.32, 68.23, 77.8). The Latin normally has a present or (82.5) future infinitive answering to the infinitive found in the revision or (34.6, 61.13) original translation; but it has a gerund or gerundive five times, with or without *ad* or *in* (33.25 quoted below, 71.6, 73.17, 78.19, 97.2; cf. the passages quoted in notes 22 and 23 below), and four times a participial or noun phrase (68.23 quoted below, 95.13, 96.18, 104.16). On two occasions the Latin does not have a corresponding expression (30.6 quoted below, 44.32 quoted above); on two others it supports about equally the reading of either version of the translation (77.8 quoted below, 147.18 quoted above).

§52. The examples show two basic patterns, e.g.,

> **CO**: ne blan (blonn **O**) *he* hwæðre *þæt he* his geongran ne
> *manode* (iuncgr[ ]de **O**) (27.4)

H: swa þeah ne geswac *he to manienne* his gingran
Ln: nec tamen discipulos suos *admonere* cessabat (1.4.17)

CO: and þa sona (ge)cigde Benedictus þa broðru (gebro[ ]
  O) him to and *heom (him O)* bebead *þæt hi (ge)namon*
  þa candele of þæs muneces handum (hondum O)
  (144.17)
  H: he þær rihte clypode þa broðru and het *geniman* þæt
  leoht of his handum
  Ln: uocatisque statim fratribus, praecepit *ei (v.l. eis)*
  lucernam de manibus *tolli* (2.20.12)

With the first type, the main clause and *þæt*-clause have the
same subject (e.g., *he* at 27.4). With the second type the clauses
have different subjects: the subject of one version's *þæt*-clause
corresponds to the accusative (e.g., *his þegnas* at 147.18 quoted
above) or dative (e.g., *heom* at 144.17 quoted here) "subject,"
sometimes unexpressed, of the other version's infinitive.[21]
Because their subject or subjects accompany only active verbs
and infinitives (e.g., at 27.4 *blan . . . manode* and *geswac . . . to
manienne*), twenty-four examples straightaway follow the first
pattern and eleven follow the second.[22] The latter differ among
themselves over the expression or nonexpression of the object:
both versions express an accusative object (70.18 [reflexive],
147.18, 169.9); one version expresses an accusative (61.13
quoted above, 109.19) or dative (144.17 quoted above) object;
neither version expresses an object, accusative or dative (78.19,
125.14, 125.16, 138.2, 138.3).[23] Passive constructions obscure
the resemblance that most of the other eleven examples, not
immediately of either of the two types, bear to the rest, e.g.,

CO: God forestihtode (forestihtade O) þæt *Abrahames sæd
  sceolde beon gemanigfealdod (gemonigfaldad O)* (55.32)
  H: God forestihtode to gemenifyldenne Abrahames sæd
  Ln: Deus *multiplicari (v.l., in Moricca, multiplicare) semen
  Abrahae* praedestinauerat (1.8.61)

The original translation has two subjects only because its
þæt-clause has a passive instead of an active construction. The
þæt-clause means **he [God] sceolde gemanifealdian Abrahames sæd*.
With the passive so transformed, the passage conforms to the
first of the patterns distinguished above:

> **CO**: **God* forestihtode *þæt he sceolde gemanigfealdian*
>   Abrahames sæd
> **H**: God forestihtode *to gemenifyldenne* Abrahames sæd

At 34.6 both of the revision's clauses must be transformed to ar-
rive at a passage of the first type: *he wæs forsewen þæt he næs
ongean gegreted* must become **he forseah hine þæt he him ongean ne
gegrette* (*he forhogode togenes gretan* **C**, om. **O**; Latin *resalutare
despiceret* [1.4.118]). And seven passages belong to the second
type after transformation, e.g.,

> **CO**: (and) *mid swiþe mycclum (micle* **O**) *ege he wearð (wear[ ]*
>   **O**) *onæled* þæt he wæs manna sawla (monna saule **O**)
>   þam ælmihtigan Gode gestreonende (gestrynende **O**)
>   (33.25)
>   **H**: eornostlice *swa micel hæte hine onælde* sawla to
>   gestrynenne Gode æmihtigum
> **Ln**: tantus quippe *illum ad collegendas* Deo animas *feruor ac-
>   cenderat* (1.4.112)

> **CO**: þa gemette heo (hio **O**) *hire hwæte ealne beon (ful)neah
>   gedæledne fram (from* **O**) *hire agenum suna* þearfendum
>   mannum (in ðearfena ælmessan **O**) (68.23)
>   **H**: þa afunde heo *þæt hire sunu hæfde* þearfum *gedæled
>   forneah eallne þone hwæte*
> **Ln**: *paene omne triticum . . .* inuenit *a filio suo* pauperibus
>   *expensum* (1.9.187)

The original translation's passive main clause and passive infinitive phrase mean **swiþe mycel ege hine onælde* and **hire agen
sunu habban . . . gedæled(ne) fulneah ealne hire hwæte* respectively,

closely matching the corresponding clauses of the revision. The main clauses of both versions of the translation have passives at 30.6, 95.13, 104.16, 104.22, and 126.24 [five times], e.g.,

CO: *se wæs gelaþod* to anes rices mannes (monnes **O**) suna
*and wæs gebeden fram (from **O**) his fæder* þæt he him
hæle gæfe (hælo agefe **O**) (30.6)

H: *se wæs gelaðod* to sumes underciniges suna hine to
gehælenne *þurh his fæder bene*

Ln: qui *inuitatus* ad filium reguli (1.4.61)

Each main clause means **his fæder gelaþode (and gebæd) hine.* Because one version has a perfect or pluperfect verb phrase rather than a passive, the final pair of examples cannot fit either pattern:

CO: þa semninga (sæmninga **O**) *wæs hie (him **O**) geþuht*
þæt þær eode fyr ut (123.27)

H: þa færinga *wæs gesewen fyr* þær of gan

Ln: exire (*v.l., in Moricca,* exire de eo) *ignis* repente *uisus
est* (2.10.4)

CO: ac he wolde *þæt for mannum (monnum **O**) gesewen wære*
þæt he betran lifes wære þonne se biscop (77.8)

H: ac he wolde *beon geþuht* swylce he bet dyde þonne se
bisceop

Ln: ut meliora quam episcopus fecisse *uideretur* (1.10.90)

The Reviser's *wæs gesewen fyr* means **[hi] gesawon fyr*; Wærferth's passive means **men gesawon þæt.* . . . The phrases *wæs . . . geþuht* and *beon geþuht* resist transformation, however, since the verb *geþyncan* cannot take an object.

Conclusion

THE REVISION WAS MADE with great care and consistency, but the original translation was excellent. The Reviser corrected—as opposed to simply altering or variegating— Wærferth's text only rarely, and in nearly every such instance our copies of the original translation may be corrupt or Wærferth may have had a corrupt Latin reading before him.

Most of the Reviser's changes make the translation more like present-day English. In fact, often the revision has the very idiom of present-day English, rather than the presumably more archaic phrasing of the original translation. It would seem, then, that many of the current features of English took shape a thousand years ago, during the tenth and early eleventh centuries.

Yet perhaps Wærferth "writ no language," and that explains why the revision seems so modern in comparison: the revision is in (more or less) unaffected English, Wærferth's original translation in some specially concocted, pseudolearned argot. But no; the original translation does not follow the Latin any more slavishly than the revision does, and all of Wærferth's constructions find parallels in other contemporary writings.

So where was the English language going? Between Wærferth's time and that of the Reviser, it may have become stricter about concord (§§2–3); the genitive continued to ease out the dative as the case of possession (§5), but for other meanings the dative replaced the instrumental (§6) and the endingless locative replaced both the dative and the instrumental (§7); the plural number superseded the dual (§8); unnecessary demonstrative pronouns were dropped from such phrases as *min þæt* and *þa þe* (§§10-11), but omitted relative pronouns were restored (§12); prepositions (§13) and verbs (§17) came to take accusative objects rather than datives; prepositions replaced cases (§14); to distinguish conjunctions from adverbs, the former were reduplicated or given the enclitic particle *þe* (§15); the auxiliary verb *gewunian* came to take *to* plus inflected infinitive, rather than a simple infinitive (§18); the verb *gemetan* came to accompany a (transitive) participle rather than an (intransitive) infinitive (§19); and resolved tenses with *habban* superseded single verbs (20.*c.*), but single verbs superseded resolved tenses with *beon/wesan* or assorted other auxiliaries (§§20-21). Out of this welter of detail note the realignment and reduction of cases (§§5-7, 13, 17) and the replacement of cases by prepositions (§14), the latter substitution being part of a wider movement away from inflections as a way of indicating meaning (§§8, 18, 20.*c.*; but cf. §§20-21).

The Reviser also deleted repetitive demonstratives or possessives (§23), subjects (§24), objects (§25), prepositions (§26), conjunctions (§27), and auxiliary verbs (§28); brought modifiers—whether adjectives, numbers, or pronouns (§32), genitive or dative phrases (§33), names (§34), predicate participles (§35), or adjective clauses (§36)—closer to their heads, and brought prepositions or postpositions closer to their objects (§37); placed auxiliary verbs after their predicate participles or adjectives (§38), but placed other verbs before predicate substantives or infinitives (§39); carefully regulated the position of the adverb *þa* (§40); and moved vocatives and interjections forward in the sentence (§41). Finally, the Reviser moved adverb clauses from before or within, to after their head clauses(§43), and replaced independent clauses with adverb or adjective clauses (§44) and all kinds of clauses with participles, adjectives, absolutes, or infinitives (§§46-52). Most of the changes enumerated in this paragraph (§§23-28, 40, 44, 46-52), as well as one mentioned in the preceding paragraph (§§10-11), evidence the Reviser's greater control and his altogether admirable wish to be concise.

Notes

Introduction

1. See for example the critical apparatus, which does not record every spelling variant, of *Homilies of Ælfric: A Supplementary Collection*, ed. John C. Pope, 2 vols., Early English Text Society 259-60 (London, 1967-68).

2. *The Two Versions of Wærferth's Translation of Gregory's "Dialogues": An Old English Thesaurus*, Toronto Old English Series 4 (Toronto, 1979).

3. Wærferth became bishop in 872 (Cyril J. R. Hart, *The Early Charters of Northern England and the North Midlands* [Leicester, 1975], pp. 363-64); Alfred's biographer, Asser, writing no later than 893, already knew of the translation and its origin (see Dorothy Whitelock, "The Prose of Alfred's Reign," in *Continuations and Beginnings*, ed. Eric G. Stanley [London, 1966], pp. 67-79). The revision's late-West-Saxon vocabulary suggests the earlier time limit, 950, and the unique manuscript of the work, Hatton 76, both establishes the later limit, 1050, and indicates the place of composition (see *Transactions of the Cambridge Bibliographical Society* 7 [1978], 245-47).

4. See Hans Hecht, *Bischof Wærferths von Worcester Übersetzung der Dialoge Gregors des Grossen: Einleitung*, Bibliothek der angelsächsischen Prosa 5:2 (Hamburg, 1907), pp. 130-83, and Helmut Gneuss, "The Origin of Standard Old English and Æthelwold's School at Winchester," *Anglo-Saxon England* 1 (1972), 63-83, esp. 80-81.

5. The Reviser freely replaced Wærferth's forms of *beon/wesan* with forms of *weorþan* (see *An Old English Thesaurus*). Today of course "to be" prevails and *weorþan* has sunk with barely a trace. So does J. M. Wattie's censure of the "duplication of passive auxiliaries" *beon/wesan* and *weorþan* as "unnecessary" and "the only false start" of the Old

English tense system apply to the language as a whole or only to certain dialects ("Tense," *Essays and Studies* 16 [1930], 143)?

6. As Fred C. Robinson has shown, the scope of the term *text* must widen here to include the syntactical glosses found in a number of Latin manuscripts ("Syntactical Glosses in Latin manuscripts of Anglo-Saxon Provenance," *Speculum* 48 [1973], 470–74).

7. Barbara M. H. Strang, *A History of English* (London, 1970), p. 75. See also William D. Whitney, *The Life and Growth of Language* (New York, 1899), pp. 157–59; George H. McKnight, *Modern English in the Making* (New York, 1928), pp. 1–4; C. L. Wrenn, *The English Language* (1949; repr., London, 1960), pp. 194–95; and D. G. Scragg, *A History of English Spelling* (Manchester, 1974), pp. 64–71.

8. Clark's assertion that "the spoken language constantly and properly modifies the written; but in any civilization rightly so called, the spoken language . . . is modified in turn and should be modified by the written language" (in Eric Partridge and John W. Clark, *British and American English since 1900* [New York, 1951], p. 214) presupposes two facts: a written standard and a way of disseminating it. And Albert C. Baugh would further argue that the second fact gives rise to the first: "The printing press, the reading habit, and all forms of communication . . . work actively towards the promotion and maintenance of a standard, especially in grammar and usage. . . . in modern times changes in grammar have been relatively slight" (*A History of the English Language* [New York, 1935], p. 248). According to Henry C. Wyld, though, "Written Standard may be said to have existed from the end of the fourteenth century, although it was not used to the complete exclusion of other forms for another hundred years or so" (*A History of Modern Colloquial English* [London, 1920], p. 5). The existence of a fourteenth-century standard may explain how Elizabeth C. Traugott, using only Chaucer and the Paston Letters as representatives of Middle English prose, could find that "from a purely syntactic point of view" early modern English lies closer to Middle English than to modern English (*A History of English Syntax* [New York, 1972], p. 2). As Wyld remarked, "When, after the introduction of printing, a definite form of English becomes the only one used in literary composition, that form is on the whole, and in essential respects, the normal descendant of Chaucer's dialect, and of Caxton's."

9. For the manuscripts and their dates see Neil R. Ker, *Catalogue of Manuscripts Containing Anglo-Saxon* (Oxford, 1957), nos. 60 (**C**: second half of the eleventh century), 96, 182 (**O**: Books I and II from the beginning of the eleventh century, III and IV from the middle), and

328 (**H**). Manuscript **C** wants a leaf from Book IV, **O** a leaf from Book III. **O** also stops abruptly in mid page about four-fifths of the way through the last book.

10. A forthcoming article by the author in *Neuphilologische Mitteilungen* deals with the differences of inflection between the two versions of the translation.

11. *Bischofs Wærferth von Worcester Übersetzung der Dialoge Gregors des Grossen*, Bibliothek der angelsächsischen Prosa 5 (Leipzig, 1900), cited hereafter as "Hecht." The major corrections to Hecht's text of manuscript **H** appear in *Anglia* 94 (1976), 163-165; to his **C**, in *Mediaevalia* 3 (1977), 165-72. For a diplomatic edition of the Canterbury fragment, unknown to Hecht, see *Anglo-Saxon England* 6 (1977), 121-35.

12. *Grégoire le Grand, Dialogues*, 3 vols., Sources chrétiennes 251, 260, and 265 (Paris, 1978-80). Umberto Moricca's edition (*Gregorii Magni Dialogi libri IV*, Fonti per la storia d'Italia 57 [Rome, 1924]) provides additional variant readings at §§13.*b.*, 20.*b.* (note 41), 34. *a.* and *b.*, 37.*a.*, 39, and 49-50 below.

13. Etsko Kruisinga, "How to Study Old English Syntax," *English Studies* 8 (1926), 48-49; Benno J. Timmer, *Studies in Bishop Wærferth's Translation of the "Dialogues" of Gregory the Great* (Wageningen, 1934), and "The Place of the Attributive Noun-Genitive in Anglo-Saxon, with Special Reference to Gregory's *Dialogues*," *English Studies* 21 (1939), 49-72.

14. Notably Morris P. Tilley, *Zur Syntax Wærferths* (Leipzig, 1903), and Hecht, *Einleitung*, pp. 37-121.

Chapter 1

1. See Hans Stoelke, *Die Inkongruenz zwischen Subjekt und Prädikat im Englischen und in den verwandten Sprachen*, Anglistische Forschungen 49 (Heidelberg, 1916), and, for additional examples from manuscripts **C** and **O** of Wærferth's translation, P. N. U. Harting, "The Text of the Old English Translation of Gregory's *Dialogues*," *Neophilologus* 22 (1937), 298, cited hereafter as "Harting."

2. Old English quotations include all the differences between manuscripts **C** and **O** except *þ/ð* variation and differences over the conjunction or prefix "and." For the conjunction, **C** and **H** always use the tironian nota *7*; **O**, in Books I and II of the translation, uses *7* or *ond* (rarely, *on*: see §46, note 9, below). At the beginning of words, **H** always uses *and*; **C** normally uses *7*, sometimes *and* or *ond*; **O** uses all

three forms freely, e.g., *andgyt, 7gites, ondgit.* Thus *sy onlihte* **C**, *se onliht*
O becomes *sy (se* **O**) *onliht(e)*; *7 gehwylce wyrte þe he ær mid* . . . **C**, *ond*
gehwelce wyrte ðe he [ ]mid . . . **O** becomes *and gehwylce (gehwelce* **O**) *wyrte*
þe he ær (def. **O**) *mid* . . . ; and so on. Latin quotations, from de
Vogüé's edition, include only those variant readings that may help explain the Old English. The abbreviation "om." means "omitted";
"def.," "defective"; "v.l.," "varia lectio"; "v.ll.," "variae lectiones."

3. *Sweet's Anglo-Saxon Reader,* revised by Dorothy Whitelock (1967;
repr., Oxford, 1970), p. 22, lines 148–49.

4. Tauno F. Mustanoja, *A Middle English Syntax: Part I, Parts of*
Speech, Mémoires de la Société Néophilologique de Helsinki 23
(Helsinki, 1960), pp. 95–97, 104–8, and 182.

5. Alistair Campbell, *Old English Grammar* (1959; repr., Oxford,
1971), §707.

6. 18.16, 24.18, 71.26, 79.16, 81.24, 101.2 157.7 (**O** may have a
postpositional phrase rather than a dative of possession), 169.31
[eight times]; 6.22, 20.9, 34.15, 88.1 (def. **O**). See Johann Ernst
Wülfing, *Die Syntax in den Werken Alfreds des Grossen,* 2 vols. (Bonn,
1894–1901), §§43–51 and 80–90, cited hereafter as "Wülfing."

7. Pope has documented Ælfric's near abandonment of the instrumental case (*Homilies,* 1:183–84).

8. See Wülfing, §132, and Frederic T. Visser, *An Historical Syntax of*
the English Language, 3 vols. in 4 (Leiden, 1963–73), §1150, cited
hereafter as "Visser."

9. Rudolf Krohn indicated some of the passages in which both versions of the translation have the phrase *sume dæge: Der Gebrauch des*
schwachen Adjektivs in den wichtigsten Prosaschriften der Zeit Alfreds des
Grossen (Breslau, 1914), p. 28.

10. Compare the case variations at 143.29 and 145.3 discussed in
note 18 below, and see Pope, *Homilies,* 1:183. The unique instance of
sume dæg replacing *sume dæge* occurs at one of the places where a contemporary auxiliary scribe, not the main scribe, has copied the text of
the revision (see Ker, *Catalogue,* no. 328).

11. See Karl Brunner, *Altenglische Grammatik, nach der*
Angelsächsischen Grammatik von Eduard Sievers, 3rd ed. (Tübingen,
1965), §360.2, cited hereafter as "Sievers-Brunner."

12. Mustanoja, *Syntax,* pp. 123, 125, and 157.

13. 5.23, 17.19 (*hire þæs* **C**, *þæs* **O**, *hire* **H**), 35.21, 60.22, 64.27,
65.14, 90.9, 141.20, 155.11; see Rudolf Vleeskruyer, *The Life of St.*
Chad: An Old English Homily (Amsterdam, 1953), pp. 48 and 140
(§62). At 78.15, quoted in §40, note 27, below, both versions have *þæt*
his hors; and though Wærferth's *þæt* probably represents a

demonstrative, the Reviser's serves as a conjunction. *An Old English Thesaurus* lists the many instances of the Reviser's personal pronouns replacing Wærferth's demonstratives.

14. Bruce Mitchell has distinguished between the *se þe* relative, in which the form of *se* has the case of the adjective clause, and the *se'þe* relative, in which it has the case of the main clause ("Adjective Clauses in Old English Poetry," *Anglia* 81 [1963], 298-99). The Reviser also often uses *þe* instead of a form of *se* (see *An Old English Thesaurus*); and once, in King Alfred's brief prefatory letter to the translation, the Reviser substitutes a form of *se* for a relative of the *se þe* type (no Latin):

> **C:** us *þam þe* God swa micle heanesse worldgeþingða forgifen
> hafað is seo mæste ðearf (1.5)
> **H:** us *þam* God swa micele healicnysse woruldgeþingða
> forgifen hæfð is seo mæste þearf

Hecht reported *us: an:: god* for **H** and printed *us þam þe God*. Actually the manuscript reads *us þam gogod*, with *þ*, the last minim of *m*, and the first *go* erased. Manuscript **O** does not include a copy of Alfred's letter (Hecht 1.1–21): see Kenneth Sisam, *Studies in the History of Old English Literature* (1953; repr., Oxford, 1967), pp. 229–31, and compare §§15, note 32, and 23, note, below.

15. Wærferth's *þæs* doubtfully represents an object of *sagas(t)*, as well as of *lysteþ*, given the few possible instances of *secgan* with a genitive object cited by Visser, §391, and George Shipley, *The Genitive Case in Anglo-Saxon Poetry* (Baltimore, 1903), pp. 65–66. For the absence of relative pronoun see Wülfing, §304, and Mitchell, "Adjective Clauses," pp. 307–10.

16. See Fritz Wende, *Über die nachgestellten Präpositionen im Angelsächsischen*, Untersuchungen und Texte aus der deutschen und englischen Philologie 70 (Berlin, 1915), esp. pp. 77–80, and Mitchell, "Prepositions, Adverbs, Prepositional Adverbs, Postpositions, Separable Prefixes, or Inseparable Prefixes, in Old English?" *Neuphilologische Mitteilungen* 79 (1978), 240–57.

17. **C** and **O**'s handling of *in* and *on* constitutes one of the models for "An Elementary Way to Illuminate Detail of Textual History," *Manuscripta* 21 (1977), 38–41.

18. 16.6, 17.2, 26.15, 27.14 (**O** has *ond* instead of **C**'s *on*: cf. §46, note 9, below), 29.30, 30.10, 34.29, 38.10, 45.26, 51.33, 61.26, 65.18, 66.4 68.3, 74.29, 82.29, 125.32, 134.22, 143.29, 145.3, 169.26, 170.34 (Hecht failed to make out **O**'s prepositional object *ða*

tid), 172.17 [twenty-three times]. At 17.2, 74.29, 143.29, and 145.3, Wærferth's preposition may have an endingless locative object rather than an accusative; at 143.29 and 145.3 the revision may have an accusative. See further §7 above.

19. 15.20, 42.25, 45.29, 58.22, 73.24, 80.2, 89.11, 95.24, 114.15, 173.14 [ten times]. See Wülfing, §§688–94 and 779–820.

20. Harting listed many of the examples of *mid* with an accusative in manuscript **C** or **O** (p. 289).

21. John R. Clark Hall, *A Concise Anglo-Saxon Dictionary*, 4th ed., with a "Supplement" by Herbert D. Meritt (Cambridge, 1960), p. 126, cited hereafter as "Clark Hall-Meritt." The other comprehensive Old English dictionary does not have an entry for the word: Thomas Northcote Toller, *An Anglo-Saxon Dictionary, Based on the Manuscript Collections of the Late Joseph Bosworth* (1882–98) and *Supplement* (1908–21), with *Revised and Enlarged Addenda and Corrigenda* by Alistair Campbell (Oxford, 1972), cited hereafter as "Bosworth-Toller-Campbell."

22. Compare Mustanoja, *Syntax*, pp. 67–70 and 95–97.

23. 21.32, 55.25, 56.11, 83.2, 97.29, 101.19, 131.13, 136.11, 145.20, 152.10 [ten times]. When drawing attention to a few differences of syntax between the two versions of Wærferth's translation, Kruisinga remarked, "It is not necessary for me to illustrate the numerous cases that [*sic*] the **C**-text has an instrumental, which the Reviser . . . replaced by a dative with a preposition, they are found in plenty" ("Old English Syntax," p. 48). I have not seen Andrei Danchev's *The Parallel Use of the Synthetic Dative-Instrumental and Periphrastic Prepositional Constructions in Old English*, Annuaire de l'Université de Sofia, Faculté des Lettres 63:2 (Sofia, 1969).

24. 26.24, 32.22, 38.27, 39.4, 51.19, 72.4, 83.22, 83.32, 84.2, 86.30, 90.10, 114.22, 133.9, 145.24, 147.31, 154.16, 154.19, 158.10, 172.7.

25. Two of the prepositions find equivalent adverbs: at 15.29 the phrase *fram him* becomes *him þanon*, and at 173.11 the adverb *ufor* serves beside the revision's *hyhra ofer*. Also compare the passage quoted in note 28 below, and two passages in which the revision's locative *ham* corresponds syntactically but not in meaning to the original translation's prepositional or postpositional phrase:

CO: þæs cnihtes fæder *him fram* cyrde (30.9)
  H: þæs cnihtes fæder *ham* cyrrende
 Ln: reuertens pater (1.4.62)

CO: eft *on (to* **O***)* hire huse cyrde (cirde **O**) (68.8)
 H: eft *ham* gecyrde
Ln: reuertebatur (1.9.181)

Here, and at 89.33, *ham* may represent an adverb helping to translate
the Latin prefix *re-*.

26. Paul E. Szarmach has remarked upon another instance of an
eleventh-century scribe replacing a dative absolute with a prepositional phrase ("Vercelli Homily XX," *Mediaeval Studies* 35 [1973], 25).
See further §45, note, below.

27. The original translation may have a genitive or dative object at
117.13 instead of an accusative: **CO**'s *fandian (ondian* **O***) þæs halgan
weres willan and geornnysse (gyrnesse* **O***)* corresponds to **H**'s *andian on þæs
halgan weres gecneordnyssum* (Latin *sancti uiri studiis . . . aemulari* [2.8.8]).
When at 124.9 *þa broðru . . . ongean gecigde* replaces *þa broðru gecigde*,
translating *reuocauit* (v.l. *uocauit*) *fratres* (de Vogüé 2.10.11), rather
than functioning as a postposition, *ongean* very likely forms part of a
verb *ongeangecigan*, "call back, revoke" (cf. *ongeancigan*, accepted by
Bosworth-Toller-Campbell, *Addenda*, p. 50).

28. The Reviser's phrase *anre flane scyte* could have the dative or instrumental case, not the accusative. It corresponds to *in anes flanes
(anr[ ]nes* **O***) scyte* and translates *in (v.ll. ad, om.) unius sagittae cursum* (de
Vogüé 2.7.6).

29. See Mitchell, "Old English *'oð þæt'* Adverb?" *Notes and Queries* 25
(1978), 390–94.

30. 17.13, 42.25, 57.10, 57.18, 62.28, 69.29, 72.29, 73.30, 75.20,
77.10, 78.15, 89.19, 96.17 (om. **C**), 97.13, 123.21 (def.**O**), 126.30,
135.23, 140.8, 140.12, 145.14 (*mit ty* **O**), 156.12 (om. **C**), 164.17
[twenty-two times]. See Pope, *Homilies*, 1:102–3.

31. *Forþam þe* 8.1, 8.18, 19.8, 23.16 (**O** reads *for ðone fæstu* beside **C**'s
forþon ic efste), 29.23, 33.6, 38.15, 40.12, 56.2, 71.22, 82.9, 84.21,
89.33, 101.24, 101.29, 103.4, 158.6 [seventeen times]. See Peter S.
Baker, "The Old English Canon of Byrhtferth of Ramsey," *Speculum*
55 (1980), 25–26.

32. Alfred's letter contains a third instance of the Reviser's substitution of *þæt* for *þætte*, at 1.5 (om. **O**; see §11, note 14, above).

33. Mustanoja, *Syntax*, p. 101.

34. See Morgan Callaway, Jr., *The Infinitive in Anglo-Saxon*,
Carnegie Institution of Washington Publication 167 [read 169]
(Washington, D.C., 1913), p. 56, and Visser, §1331, as well as §21.*f.*
below.

35. For *gemetan* with infinitive or participle see Callaway, *Infinitive*, p. 116, and Visser, §§2067 (p. 2252), 2084 (p. 2342), and 2114 (p. 2380); for the change from transitive verb to intransitive, see note 41 below.

36. Manfred Scheler cited most of the examples in his dissertation *Altenglische Lehnsyntax* (Berlin, 1961), p. 56. See also Wattie, "Tense," pp. 134–39; Visser, §§1771–1889; and Gerhard Nickel, *Die "Expanded Form" im Altenglischen*, Kieler Beiträge zur Anglistik und Amerikanistik 3 (Neumünster, 1966). Simeon Potter observed that the revision "has less liking for the periphrastic past tense with *wesan* (in 34 places rejected), but generally retains that with *onginnan* (in 3 places rejected; retained in 16)" ("On the Relation of the Old English Bede to Wærferth's Gregory and to Alfred's Translations," in *Mémoires de la Société Royale des Sciences de Bohême, Classe des Lettres* 1930 [Prague, 1931], p. 39); see further §21.*d.* below.

37. According to Josef Raith, elsewhere in the original translation, "einfache Deponensformen werden . . . nicht umschrieben" (*Untersuchungen zum englischen Aspekt*, Studien und Texte zur englischen Philologie 1 [Munich, 1951], p. 50). Perhaps Wærferth's copy of the *Dialogues* read *testatus*.

38. The Latin has a present participle for the Old English examples at 22.25, 30.2, 68.10, 72.17, 72.19, 80.14, and 170.31 [seven times]; a perfect participle for those at 65.20 and 97.24.

39. The Latin has a present form of *sum* for the Old English examples at 34.33, 55.18, 57.32, 67.17, 80.29, 96.21, 100.27, 105.15, 127.4, 127.20, 129.28, 142.12, 143.8, 143.11, 148.29 (past participle **C**), 171.9, and 172.26 [seventeen times]; a pluperfect form for those at 22.13, 96.16, 131.21, and 140.9. Because of manuscript **C**'s reading, the example at 148.29 appears in the next paragraph as well.

40. See Wattie, "Tense," pp. 132–34 and 139–42, and Visser, §§1890–2000. Wærferth and the Reviser read the Latin differently in a third example:

> **CO**: swyþe ungerisenlic (swiðe ungerysenlic **O**) me þynceþ (þinceð **O**) þæt þæt wære þæt . . . (136.23)
>
> **H**: swyðe unþæslic mæg *beon geþuht* þæt . . .
>
> **Ln**: ualde enim *esse* inconueniens *uidetur* (2.16.32)

The earlier writer construes *esse* with *inconueniens*, the later writer construes it with *videtur*. For the use of *mæg beon* instead of *wære*, see §21.*c.* below.

41. Latin variants can account for the nonce examples at 88.34 and 132.17 of the same subject accompanying both the passive verb phrases *nelle . . . beon geswenced* and *beon . . . upp aræred* (**CO**) and the intransitive verbs *swinc* and *upp arisan* (**H**): the passives *noli fatigari* (1.12.17) and *erigi* (2.15.4) found in some manuscripts of the *Dialogues* agree with the original translation, while the readings of other manuscripts, the active verbs *noli fatigare* and *erigere* (the latter cited as a variant only in Moricca's edition), support the revision. Compare the passage quoted in §19 above, and for Wærferth's use of the modal auxiliary *nelle* at 88.34, see §21.*b.* below.

42. See Wattie, "Tense," pp. 130–32, and Visser, §§2001–54.

43. See Visser, §§1174–1371 and 1483–1734.

44. At 147.18, quoted in §51 below, the Reviser transfers the auxiliary from a dependent clause to the main clause.

Chapter 2

1. Alfred's letter includes another example of the variation found a few pages later at 7.24 in the translation proper: ðam *godcundan and* þam *gastlican rihte* **C**, þam *godcundum and gastlicum rihte* **H** (1.11; see §11, note 14, above).

2. For this passage see further §43 below. *Hit* precedes the accusative *þæt*-clause of the first sentence quoted in §51 and precedes most of the nominative *þæt*-clauses cited in §24.*b.* At 39.4, quoted in §27.*a.*, Wærferth uses the conjunction *þæt*, not the pronoun.

3. Hecht reported *[ ]hymnum* for manuscript **O** at 169.13, but read *[ ]n ymnum*, beside **C**'s *on ymnum*. Mustanoja has concluded, "It is possible that the repetition of a preposition after a conjunction and the like is somewhat more common in M[iddle] E[nglish] than it is in the present-day, but the matter is complicated by the fact that even in prose repetition of this kind seems to be largely dependent on the writer's personal style" (*Syntax*, p. 347).

Chapter 3

1. Compare Charles Carlton, "Word Order of Noun Modifiers in Old English Prose," *Journal of English and Germanic Philology* 62 (1963), 778–83, and H. Harwood Hess, "Old English Nominals," *Papers on Language and Literature* 6 (1970), 302–13.

2. Neither Clark Hall-Meritt nor Bosworth-Toller-Campbell allows any exceptions.

3. See Visser, §1156 (p. 1274), and Mustanoja, *Syntax*, pp. 116–17.

4. Alfred Reszkiewicz has discussed split constructions in Old English, when the modifier consists of an adjective clause, an appositive name, a genitive, or an emphatic pronoun ("Split Constructions in Old English," in *Studies in Language and Literature in Honour of Margaret Schlauch*, ed. Mieczysław Brahmer, Stanisław Helszytński, and Julian Krzyżanowski [Warsaw, 1966], pp. 317–18).

5. Compare the analysis of the position of these pronouns or adjectives by William H. Brown, Jr., *A Syntax of King Alfred's "Pastoral Care,"* Janua linguarum, series practica 101 (The Hague, 1970), pp. 41–42, and see §35.*b.* below for three passages in which Wærferth's predicate participle or adjective corresponds to the Reviser's attributive.

6. Matti Rissanen has discussed the different meanings of *an* (*The Uses of "One" in Old and Early Middle English*, Mémoires de la Société Néophilologique de Helsinki 31 [Helsinki, 1967], pp. 134–35); Mustanoja has discussed the position of the adjective "almighty" ("*Almighty* in Early English: A Study in Positional Syntax," in *Festschrift Prof. Dr. Herbert Koziol zum siebzigsten Geburtstag*, ed. Gero Bauer, Frank K. Stanzel, and Frank Zaic, Wiener Beiträge zur englischen Philologie 75 [Vienna, 1973], pp. 204–12).

7. Timmer ("Place of the Attributive") gave the total number of attributive genitives for the original translation and the total number for the revision, but he cited or quoted only a fraction of the examples and did not distinguish those in which the two versions differ over the position of the attributive.

8. The revision's attributive precedes its head fifty-eight times with the Latin (8.16 [om. **C**], 18.26, 19.33, 19.35, 20.21, 26.6, 33.21, 38.25, 39.12, 40.7, 58.35, 69.26, 72.29, 75.23, 76.17, 78.9, 85.32, 86.29, 96.1, 96.28, 100.30, 101.16, 101.17, 103.34, 105.28, 106.8, 107.17, 107.31 [def.**O**], 108.19, 113.20, 113.28, 117.9, 117.11, 117.28, 123.29, 124.13, 124.24, 124.25, 130.9, 134.9, 139.32, 140.8, 142.23, 146.9, 146.31, 150.18, 151.1, 151.30, 162.11, 162.21, 169.30, 170.5, 170.17, 171.12 [Hecht printed *sunnanleoman* for the revision, instead of genitive *sunnan* plus head word *leoman*], 171.16, 171.27, 173.12, 173.33), thirty-nine times against the Latin (8.8, 18.28, 19.6, 19.12, 20.16, 21.26, 22.9, 22.10, 29.2, 30.1, 30.2, 34.26, 34.30, 43.30, 50.16, 50.23, 51.13, 55.7, 58.28, 59.30, 59.31, 64.14, 70.7, 72.21, 72.24, 84.3, 96.31, 101.23, 102.24, 103.11, 107.13, 113.24, 125.12, 126.20, 127.17, 133.15, 137.2, 149.14,

173.4), and thirteen times neither with nor against (3.20, 29.6, 40.19, 76.10, 87.24, 87.25, 106.27, 109.27, 114.25, 125.5, 140.29, 141.8, 143.1 [def. **O**]). Wærferth's attributive precedes its head seven times with the Latin (32.32, 33.30, 89.29, 130.7, 134.16, 138.34, 140.5), ten times against (26.12, 36.29, 51.24, 56.32, 103.3, 116.27, 127.30, 133.21, 142.21, 151.23), once neither with nor against (23.23). The manuscripts of the original translation themselves once differ over the position of an attributive genitive: at 17.12 the genitive precedes its head in manuscript **O** but follows in **C**, the revision, and the Latin. In still another passage two attributives exchange position:

CO: *Bonefacies (Bonifatius* **O***)* w(e)orce *þæs bisc(e)opes* (61.24)

H: *þæs bisceopes* weorce *Bonefaties*

Ln: *Bonifatii episcopi opere* (1.9.81)

See further §34.*b*. below.

9. Compare Brown, *A Syntax*, pp. 50–51. At 19.34 each version has the dative attributive *him sylfum*; the other six examples involve genitives.

10. Compare the Reviser's substitution of *ealdor wæpnedmanna* for *wera ealdorman* at 27.1 (discussed by Timmer, "Place of the Attributive," p. 55), and observe Hecht's word division at 171.12, quoted in note 8 above.

11. Eilert Ekwall cited several instances from other Old English texts of "members of the group [genitive] separated by the governing word" ("Studies on the Genitives of Groups in English," in *Bulletin de la Société Royale des Lettres de Lund* 1942–43 [Lund, 1943], pp. 4–6).

12. 19.17, 41.30, 43.30 (quoted in the preceding pargraph), 56.21, 57.11, 61.24 (quoted in §33.*b.*, note 8), 61.27, 69.29, 96.5, 97.13, 98.2, 124.23, 130.19, 131.11, 133.15 [fifteen times]. Niilo Peltola's study, "On Appositional Constructions in Old English Prose," includes many quotations from Wærferth's original translation but ignores the revision (*Neuphilologische Mitteilungen* 61 [1960], 159–203).

13. Compare Robinson, "Syntactical Glosses," p. 473 and fn. 104, and see §32.*b*. above.

14. See Callaway, *The Absolute Participle in Anglo-Saxon* (Baltimore, 1889).

15. The revision parallels the Latin just under half the time, in thirty-one of sixty-three passages: 6.7, 15.14, 15.31, 23.18, 27.14 (om.**C**), 33.18, 36.29, 43.9, 51.10, 56.21, 58.35, 59.12, 61.22, 63.16, 64.29, 73.27, 76.10, 76.13, 77.10, 81.16 (Hecht punctuated the original translation for an independent rather than an adjective

clause), 81.31, 82.3, 85.29, 95.17, 124.9, 129.24 (def.**O**), 135.20, 151.31, 163.21, 163.35, 171.5. Otherwise the Latin supports the original translation (7.21, 25.25, 28.10, 30.10, 36.33, 52.22 [om.**O**], 53.21, 53.30, 69.3, 79.10, 80.3 [om. **O**], 97.26, 128.9, 130.31, 137.2, 139.12, 155.16, 157.2, 157.18, 162.11, 172.17 [twenty-one times]) or neither version (5.14, 23.20 [def. **O**], 26.3, 43.15, 50.27, 50.32, 76.29, 84.21, 107.19, 109.15, 169.20 [eleven times]). The revision does not exhibit the "strong tendency" alleged for Old English by David Carkeet "to avoid sentences in which a relative clause intervenes between constituents of the main clause" ("Old English Correlatives: An Exercise in Internal Syntactic Reconstruction," *Glossa* 10 [1976], 44). Timmer cited a little over a third of the examples (*Studies*, pp. 24–25).

16. See Mitchell, "Adjective Clauses," pp. 298–99.

17. The Latin supports the original translation four times (46.1, 80.1, 80.23, 125.1), neither version twice (34.3, 173.19).

18. 34.3, 36.16, 39.5, 41.20, 73.27, 73.31, 78.3 (om. **C**), 79.13, 83.12, 105.15, 116.8, 124.33 (def. **O**), 131.19 (the particle lies closer to its object in the original translation), 138.33, 155.4 (**O** reads *to cwæð* with **C** and **H**, not the *acwæð* reported by Hecht) [fifteen times]. The particles at 36.16, 78.3, and 138.33 Hecht printed as verbal prefixes, the rest as postpositions: see §13.*a.* above.

19. 7.6, 17.22, 21.34, 22.21, 24.5 (quoted in the next note), 25.13, 28.10, 32.9, 38.1 (om. **O**), 38.14, 39.10, 39.14, 40.2, 59.14 (om. **C**; **O** has *in ða he*, not *in þa þe he* as implied by Hecht's critical apparatus), 64.30, 80.13, 80.15, 81.17, 82.16, 89.31, 105.15, 116.1, 125.18 (def. **O**), 127.8, 128.10, 132.2, 132.15 (om. **C**), 136.2, 138.26, 141.15 (def. **O**), 142.5, 144.7, 149.4, 156.11, 170.2 [thirty-five times]. Timmer cited a majority of the examples (*Studies*, pp. 92–101); see also Wende, *Präpositionen*, and Mitchell, "Prepositions."

20. At 24.5, where *þære he wæs bebeodende (bebeodenne* **O***) and þus to hire cwæð* becomes *þære he bebeodende þus to cwæð*, the original translation has both demonstrative *þære* (used as a relative) and personal pronoun *hire*, the revision only *þære* (Latin *cui praecipiens dixit* [1.3.14]). See further §46 below.

21. 3.9, 5.32 (def.**O**), 7.17, 15.2, 16.1, 16.13, 16.29, 22.24, 25.34, 29.21, 30.26, 32.34, 33.13, 40.31, 42.7, 45.2, 46.23, 54.5, 55.18, 55.27, 62.28, 63.17, 66.26, 68.18, 68.26, 76.18, 77.8, 80.24 (om. **C**), 106.25, 107.19, 118.11, 131.19, 136.14, 143.15, 148.3, 148.23, 172.10 [thirty-seven times]; Wærferth puts the auxiliary first at 39.5, 46.4, 89.13, and 146.10. Timmer cited half a dozen of the passages, to show that in general manuscript "**H** tends towards front-position"

of the verb "to be" (*Studies*, pp. 44–45). Visser has discussed each type of construction: *beon/wesan* with predicate adjective (§§241–47), present participle (§§1800–89), or past participle (§§289, 1145–47, and 1898–1904); *weorþan* with adjective (§234, p. 208) or participle (§§1798–99 and 1897); *habban* with past participle (§§2001–54). See also Nickel, *Die "Expanded Form,"* passim; Carlton, *Descriptive Syntax of the Old English Charters*, Janua linguarum, series practica 111 (The Hague, 1970), pp. 163–67; and Harvey Minkoff, "An Example of Lating [read *Latin*] Influence on Ælfric's Translation Style," *Neophilologus* 61 (1977), 127–42.

22. At 66.26 the original translation reads *hit wæs to ongitanne þæt (and* **O**) . . . *þæt win . . . weaxende wære* beside the revision's *þæt win . . . wære akenned weaxende* (quoted more fully, with the Latin, in §47 below).

23. Sievers-Brunner, §§420.1 and 422.5. Compare the two clauses with *an(a)* discussed in the next paragraph.

24. Hecht printed *andlyf[ ]*, failing to make out the last two letters of *andlyfne*, as well as the two yoghs. When Henry Johnson transcribed **O**'s text of the translation in 1882, however, he reported *andlyf[ ]g[ ]* and suggested *andlyfne gegearwode* as the original reading (p. 51 of Johnson's unpublished transcript, among the Chase-Johnson Papers, Bowdoin College Library, Brunswick, Maine: see "A Neglected Transcript of the Cotton Manuscript of Wærferth's Old English Translation of Gregory's *Dialogues*," *Neuphilologische Mitteilungen* 79 [1978], 21–22).

25. 3.9, 5.32 (as v.l.), 30.26, 39.5, 40.31, 42.7, 45.2, 54.5, 55.18, 62.28, 63.17, 68.18, 76.18, 107.19, 136.14, 146.10 [sixteen times].

26. The number, *an*, probably means "one" at 138.15, "alone" at 3.15: compare §§32.*b*. and 38 above. Timmer cited the passages at 15.9 and 146.2 (*Studies*, pp. 44–45); for examples from other texts see Visser, §§251–60 (*beon/wesan* with a predicate noun or noun phrase), 248 (with a number), and 290, 916–23, and 1373–76 (with an infinitive).

27. Compare another passage:

CO: þa se ylca (ilca **O**) þeg(e)n þæt his hors þe he geseah acyr-
red fram (acirred from **O**) his wedendra heorta
(wedenheortnesse **O**) mid swa hrædlicum (hrædlice **O**)
bebode þæs halgan wundres, he *þa* bebead þæt man þam
(mon ðam ilcan **O**) halgan were þæt ilce hors eft
brin(c)gan sceolde (78.15)

H: þa þa se ilca þegen geseah þæt his hors wæs awended fram

his wodnysse mid swa hrædlicum bebode þæs wundres, þa
geteohhode he hit to forgifenne þam ylcan halgan were

Ln: tunc isdem miles equum suum, quem celerrimo miraculi
imperio a sua uesania uidit inmutatum, eidem sancto uiro
decreuit offerendum (1.10.107)

Wærferth, following the Latin almost word for word, does not use a
subordinate temporal clause: see further the close of §47 below.
Robert Foster has discussed the particle's stylistic effect ("The Use of
þa in Old and Middle English Narratives," *Neuphilologische Mitteilungen*
76 [1975], 404–14).

28. The two odd examples occur at 24.2 and 141.28. In the latter
Wærferth's *þa* may represent a pronoun, "those," rather than the
adverb. Neither writer uses *and* or *ac* at 16.22 (Hecht mistakenly
reported *þær* instead of *þa* for manuscript **H**), 21.10, 24.9, 24.24,
25.3, 25.13 (def. **O**), 34.23, 38.18, 46.1, 62.24, 64.11, 64.26, 68.27,
70.10, 72.20, 74.7, 78.21, 78.24, 80.23, 80.28, 81.28, 82.12, 82.22,
84.3, 85.13 (om. **O**), 88.5, 114.15, 114.28, 114.31, 115.1, 118.26,
124.7, 124.29, 125.1, 125.8, 125.16, 126.7, 131.31, 135.31, 141.28,
141.30, 142.13, 147.20, 147.26, 154.26, 157.10, and 171.22 [forty-
seven times]; both do so at 15.30, 18.27, 35.34 (om. **O**), 39.22, 52.9,
58.15, 74.22, 82.34, 103.25 (om. **C**), and 141.5 [ten times]; only
Wærferth does so at 24.2, 38.23, 52.25, 75.1 (om. **C**), 89.6, 118.1,
132.15, and 164.1 [eight times]; and at 67.10 only the Reviser does
so.

29. Clauses begin with *tunc* (21.22, 38.18, 39.22, 74.7, 80.23,
81.28, 118.26, 125.16, 142.13, 154.26, 171.22 [eleven times]) and
cum(-) (46.1, 68.27, 74.22, 84.3). *Autem* (115.1), *cum* or *dum* (78.21,
88.5, 132.15, 151.28), *itaque* (82.12), and *vero* (126.7) come later in
other clauses.

Chapter 4

1. The adverb clause precedes in the original translation eleven times,
governed by *forðon þe* (20.1, 138.28), *gif* (139.31), *swa (. . .) swa* or *swa*
(59.22, 62.11, 117.3, 139.2 [quoted in §25.*b.* above], 148.26 [five
times]), and *þonne* or *þa þa* (61.33, 106.10, 146.13), and lies within
eight times, governed by *swa (swa)* or *sona swa* (22.11, 57.27, 101.31,
140.15, 154.16, 158.28 [six times]), *þeah* (29.30, om. **C**; quoted in
§34.*a.* above), and *(to þan) þæt* (137.6).

2. Compare Robinson's findings: "Complex sentences in Old
English prose occur sometimes with the subordinate clause preceding

the main clause, sometimes with the main clause preceding. Adverbial clauses are particularly free in this respect, and hence we might well conclude that for an Anglo-Saxon the positioning of the clause carried no stylistic effect at all. And yet, the syntactical glosses examined thus far are remarkable for the frequency with which they consign the subordinate adverbial clause to the second position, giving first place to the main clause. Could it be, then, that despite the statistical frequency of introductory adverbial clauses, these were nonetheless apprehended as being somewhat less natural syntactically than the postponed clauses and hence implied a slight elevation of stylistic level?" ("Syntactical Glosses," p. 472). See also Faith F. Gardner, *An Analysis of Syntactic Patterns of Old English*, Janua linguarum, series practica 140 (The Hague, 1971), pp. 70–74.

3. The Reviser's adverb clauses occur at 3.24, 26.21, 31.3, 41.28, 42.24, 44.9, 69.10, 86.31, 89.10, 89.27, 90.7, 95.3, and 140.8; his adjective clauses at 73.20 and 140.31. Many similarly placed clauses, of either version of the translation, begin with *þa* or a form of *se*; but *þa* may represent the adverb, not the conjunction, and the forms of *se* may function as independent demonstratives rather than as relative pronouns.

4. "Syntactical Glosses," p. 471. On parataxis and hypotaxis see also Cornelis Sprockel, *The Language of the Parker Chronicle*, 2 vols. (The Hague, 1965–73), 2:71–77.

5. According to Potter, the Reviser of Wærferth's translation "has less liking for the Dative Absolute Construction"; "one half of the Dative Absolutes [of the original translation] are retained" ("The Old English Bede," p. 39 and fn. 7). Actually the Reviser adds more absolutes than he leaves out. Of the more than eighty dative or (169.19, quoted in §6.*b.* above) instrumental absolutes that Tilley found in the original translation, twenty-three occur in those parts of the text that also survive in manuscript **H** of the revision (*Zur Syntax Wærferths,* pp. 80–84). To the twenty-three add those at 52.4, 94.15, and 133.1 (om. **C**; quoted in note 16 below). The Reviser keeps twenty-one of these absolute constructions and substitutes prepositional phrases for the remaining five (52.4, 53.10, 94.15, 118.27[twice]: see §14.*d.* above). At twelve other places, however, cited below in §§49–50, he introduces dative absolutes to replace Wærferth's clauses, for a net gain of seven. Harting remarked justly, in connection with another of Potter's statements about the translation, "His essay is stimulating, but his sweeping results are founded on too insecure a basis of facts" (p. 286).

6. 24.4, 32.26, 35.1, 36.24, 36.28, 62.16, 78.23, 78.25, 82.7,

103.30, 107.14, 114.17, 118.22, 124.32, 131.29, 135.7, 135.27, 143.10, 154.12, 170.32. Scheler (*Lehnsyntax*, p. 56) cited seven of these, as well as that at 66.26 quoted in the next paragraph. See Callaway, "The Appositive Participle in Anglo-Saxon," *Publications of the Modern Language Association* 16 (1901), 141–360.

7. At 36.24 the revision's participle *cyssende* corresponds to the original translation's second clause *and (ða) wæs cyssende*, but the participle does not come at the end of its own clause.

8. All eight examples of §49 below follow this pattern.

9. Manuscript **O** has the reduced form *on* for *ond* at 143.10: see Harting, p. 287, and compare §13, note 18, above. The same manuscript repeats the subject at 103.30 only because its scribe wrote *he mælde* in error for *hit eldode*, **C**'s reading, or the like.

10. Manuscript **H** actually has *and þus cw̄eðende*, with the standard mark of abbreviation, a straight horizontal line, over the wen. Since the scribe often writes *cw̄* for *cwæð*, perhaps we should read **and þus cwæð*. Hecht reported *þus cweðende*, missing *and* (i.e., the tironian nota 7), as well as the abbreviation mark.

11. Josephine M. Burnham quoted a similar example from Wærferth's translation of *swa* acting as "a rather characterless connective, shading into concession, result, or manner. . . . *swa*, with a tinge of concessive meaning, translates a Latin word whose application in the original was vague" (*Concessive Constructions in Old English Prose*, Yale Studies in English 39 [New York, 1911], pp. 15–16, quoting the passage at Hecht 61.6 shared by all three manuscripts **C**, **O**, and **H**).

12. See Mitchell, "Some Problems Involving Old English Periphrases with *beon/wesan* and the Present Participle," *Neuphilologische Mitteilungen* 77 (1976), 478–91.

13. See Else von Schaubert, *Vorkommen, gebietsmässige Verbreitung, und Herkunft altenglischer absoluter Partizipialkonstruktionen in Nominativ und Akkusativ* (Paderborn, 1954).

14. Von Schaubert neglected to include the specimen in her study of nominative and accusative absolutes. Compare the inflections given to some predicate participles that follow accusative singular masculine nouns: *hangiende* **CO**, *hangiendne* **H** (24.32, cited by Kruisinga, "Old English Syntax," p. 49); *cyrrende and . . . berende* **CO**, *yrnendne and . . . berendne* **H** (37.3, Hecht printed *yrnende*); *byfiende and brodettendne* **C**, *bifiende and brocciende* **O**, *cwakiendne and broddettendne* (last *n* added above the line) **H** (156.20).

15. Perhaps the scribe of manuscript **C** or an exemplar could not tolerate the uncompromisingly accusative phrase *þone abbud* in an ab-

solute construction but passed over *gangende* with its "notoriously ambiguous" ending *e*. See further §6.*b.* above.

16. The almost identical variation once occurs between the two manuscripts of the original translation, with the revision sharing **O**'s absolute:

> **C**: *þa se cyng þas word hæfde gehered,* he wæs swiðlice abreged (133.1)
>
> **O**: *gehyrdum þi[ ]m wordum,* se cining wæs swyðlice abreged
>
> **H**: *ðysum wordum þa gehyredum,* se cyning wearð swiðe þearle ablycged
>
> **Ln**: *quibus auditis,* rex uehementer territus (2.15.12)

See further §§20.*c.* and 35.*b.* above.

17. 27.4, 30.6, 33.25, 40.26, 44.32, 52.20, 55.32, 66.23, 69.25, 70.18 (def. **O**), 71.6, 73.17, 76.25, 77.8, 78.19, 78.21, 78.28, 82.5, 85.35, 95.13, 96.18, 97.2, 101.7, 104.16, 104.22, 109.19, 117.31, 123.27, 125.14, 125.16, 126.24, 128.30, 131.33, 133.17, 135.33, 136.8, 138.2, 138.3, 144.17, 147.18, 155.32, 163.16, 169.9 [forty-three times]. Kruisinga quoted the examples at 27.4 and 40.26 ("Old English Syntax," pp. 48–49). Such uses of the infinitive have received extensive study from Callaway, *Infinitive*; Hellmut Bock, "Studien zum präpositionalen Infinitiv und Akkusativ mit dem *to*-Infinitiv," *Anglia* 55 (1931), 114–249; and Visser, vol. 3.

18. Compare the adverb clause governed by *swa* quoted in note 22 below, and see Hubert G. Shearin, *The Expression of Purpose in Old English Prose*, Yale Studies in English 18 (New York, 1903), pp. 8–31 and 54–68.

19. See Callaway, *The Consecutive Subjunctive in Old English*, Modern Language Association of America Monograph Series 4 (Boston, 1933), pp. 12–27.

20. Three of the verbs consist of a form of *beon/wesan* or *weorþan*: once with a present participle (*wæs gestreonende* at 33.25 quoted below), once with a prepositional phrase (*byþ butan wæstme* at 109.19, def.**O**), and once alone (the revision's *gewurde*, at 61.13 quoted above). Wærferth uses the auxiliaries *sceolan* (78.19, 95.13, 104.22, 125.14, 125.16, 128.30, 147.18 [seven times]), *willan* or *nellan* (44.32, 78.21, 78.28, 82.5, 155.32 [five times]), and *magan* (71.6, 97.2). At 55.32 quoted below, his *þæt*-clause contains the passive expression *sceolde beon gemanigfealdod*.

21. See Ann H. Stewart, "The Old English 'Passive' Infinitive,"

Journal of English Linguistics 7 (1973), 57–68.

22. Compare a passage in which an infinitive phrase replaces an adverb clause governed by *swa*:

> **CO**: þa ongunnon hi(o) weorpan (wurpan **O**) wæter (on) and
> hlydan *swa þa doð þe fyr and bryne dwæsc(e)að* (123.32)
> **H**: ða broðru þa mid gehlyde wurpon wæter on þæt fyr *swylce
> hit to adwæscenne*
> **Ln**: cumque iaciendo aquam et ignem *quasi extinguendo*
> perstreperent (2.10.7)

Even though it has only active verbs, the original translation shifts from the subject *hi(o)*, "they [the brothers]," to *þa . . . þe*, "those [others] who."

23. At 138.2 and 138.3, instead of an object supply an unexpressed dative predicate, namely the indefinite pronoun *men*, for the verb *is* or *sy*. And supply the same predicate when an infinitive phrase replaces an adjective clause:

> **CO**: þa wæs þær hwylchugu (hwylchwega **O**) ylding þære tide
> *þe man (mon **O**) sceolde þa licþe(g)nunge and þa gedafenu þære
> byrgen(n)e gefyllan and gyldan (gieldan **O**)* (84.4)
> **H**: ðær wæs þa sumre tide ylding *to gefyllanne þa licþenunge his
> bebyrginge*
> **Ln**: cumque mora esset temporis *ad explendum debitum sepulturae*
> (1.10.193)

Men can go almost anywhere before the adjective clause or infinitive phrase.

Bibliography

Baker, Peter S. "The Old English Canon of Byrhtferth of Ramsey." *Speculum* 55 (1980), 22–37.

Baugh, Albert C. *A History of the English Language.* New York, 1935.

Bock, Hellmut. "Studien zum präpositionalen Infinitiv und Akkusativ mit dem *to*-Infinitiv." *Anglia* 55 (1931), 114–249.

Bosworth, Joseph. See Toller.

Brown, William H., Jr. *A Syntax of King Alfred's "Pastoral Care."* Janua linguarum, series practica 101. The Hague, 1970.

Brunner, Karl. *Altenglische Grammatik, nach der Angelsächsischen Grammatik von Eduard Sievers.* 3rd ed. Tübingen, 1965. [Sievers-Brunner]

Burnham, Josephine M. *Concessive Constructions in Old English Prose.* Yale Studies in English 39. New York, 1911.

Callaway, Morgan, Jr. *The Absolute Participle in Anglo-Saxon.* Baltimore, 1889.

———. "The Appositive Participle in Anglo Saxon." *Publications of the Modern Language Association* 16 (1901), 141–360.

———. *The Consecutive Subjunctive in Old English.* Modern Language Association of America Monograph Series 4. Boston, 1933.

———. *The Infinitive in Anglo-Saxon.* Carnegie Institution of Washington Publication 167 [read 169]. Washington, D.C., 1913.

Campbell, Alistair. *Old English Grammar*. 1959. Repr., with corrections, Oxford, 1971.

———. See Toller.

Carkeet, David. "Old English Correlatives: An Exercise in Internal Syntactic Reconstruction." *Glossa* 10 (1976), 44–63.

Carlton, Charles. *Descriptive Syntax of the Old English Charters*. Janua linguarum, series practica 111. The Hague, 1970.

———. "Word Order of Noun Modifiers in Old English Prose." *Journal of English and Germanic Philology* 62 (1963), 778–83.

Clark, John W. See Partridge.

Clark Hall, John R. *A Concise Anglo-Saxon Dictionary*. 4th ed., with a "Supplement" by Herbert D. Meritt. Cambridge, 1960. [Clark Hall-Meritt]

Danchev, Andrei. *The Parallel Use of the Synthetic Dative-Instrumental and Periphrastic Prepositional Constructions in Old English*. Annuaire de l'Université de Sofia, Faculté des Lettres 63:2. Sofia, 1969.

de Vogüé, Adalbert, ed. *Grégoire le Grand, Dialogues*. 3 vols. Sources chrétiennes 251, 260, and 265. Paris, 1978–80.

Ekwall, Eilert. "Studies on the Genitive of Groups in English." In *Bulletin de la Société Royale des Lettres de Lund* 1942–43. Lund, 1943, pp. 1–104.

Foster, Robert. "The Use of *þa* in Old and Middle English Narratives." *Neuphilologische Mitteilungen* 76 (1975), 404–14.

Gardner, Faith F. *An Analysis of Syntactic Patterns of Old English*. Janua linguarum, series practica 140. The Hague, 1971.

Gneuss, Helmut. "The Origin of Standard Old English and Æthelwold's School at Winchester." *Anglo-Saxon England* 1 (1972), 63–83.

Hall. See Clark Hall.

Hart, Cyril J. R. *The Early Charters of Northern England and the North Midlands*. Leicester, 1975.

Harting, P. N. U. "The Text of the Old English Translation of Gregory's *Dialogues*." *Neophilologus* 22 (1937), 281–302.

Hecht, Hans, ed. *Bischofs Wærferth von Worcester Übersetzung der Dialoge Gregors des Grossen*. Bibliothek der angelsächsischen Prosa 5. Leipzig, 1900. Repr., except for pp. 351–74 containing lists of manuscript accents, Darmstadt, 1965.

————. *Bischof Wærferths von Worcester Übersetzung der Dialoge Gregors des Grossen: Einleitung*. Bibliothek der angelsächsischen Prosa 5:2. Hamburg, 1907. Repr. with the above item, Darmstadt, 1965.

Hess, H. Harwood. "Old English Nominals." *Papers on Language and Literature* 6 (1970), 302–13.

Johnson, Henry. "COTTON Ms. OTHO, C, I. Part II. Copy 1882–3. St. Grecokys [*sic*] Dialogues." Brunswick, Maine. Bowdoin College Library. Chase-Johnson Collection. [Transcript made in 1882 of fols. 1–137 of British Library, Cotton Otho C.i, vol. 2, with variant readings added in 1883 from Corpus Christi College, Cambridge 322.]

Ker, Neil R. *Catalogue of Manuscripts Containing Anglo-Saxon*. Oxford, 1957.

Krohn, Rudolf. *Der Gebrauch des schwachen Adjektivs in den wichtigsten Prosaschriften der Zeit Alfreds des Grossen*. Breslau, 1914.

Kruisinga, Etsko. "How to Study Old English Syntax." *English Studies* 8 (1926), 44–49.

McKnight, George H. *Modern English in the Making*. New York, 1928.

Meritt, Herbert D. See Clark Hall.

Minkoff, Harvey. "An Example of Lating [read *Latin*] Influence on Ælfric's Translation Style." *Neophilologus* 61 (1977), 127–42.

Mitchell, Bruce. "Adjective Clauses in Old English Poetry." *Anglia* 81 (1963), 298–322.

————. "Old English 'oð þæt' Adverb?" *Notes and Queries* 25 (1978), 390–94.

————. "Prepositions, Adverbs, Prepositional Adverbs, Postpositions, Separable Prefixes, or Inseparable Prefixes, in Old English?" *Neuphilologische Mitteilungen* 79 (1978), 240–57.

————. "Some Problems Involving Old English Periphrases

with *beon/wesan* and the Present Participle." *Neuphilologische Mitteilungen* 77 (1976), 478–91.

Moricca, Umberto, ed. *Gregorii Magni Dialogi libri IV*. Fonti per la storia d'Italia 57. Rome, 1924.

Mustanoja, Tauno F. *"Almighty* in Early English: A Study in Positional Syntax." In *Festschrift Prof. Dr. Herbert Koziol zum siebzigsten Geburtstag*, ed. Gero Bauer, Frank K. Stanzel, and Frank Zaic. Wiener Beiträge zur englischen Philologie 75. Vienna, 1973, pp. 204–12.

———. *A Middle English Syntax: Part I, Parts of Speech*. Mémoires de la Société Néophilologique de Helsinki 23. Helsinki, 1960.

Nickel, Gerhard. *Die "Expanded Form" im Altenglischen*. Kieler Beiträge zur Anglistik und Amerikanistik 3. Neumünster, 1966.

Partidge, Eric, and Clark, John W. *British and American English since 1900*. New York, 1951.

Peltola, Niilo. "On Appositional Constructions in Old English Prose." *Neuphilologische Mitteilungen* 61 (1960), 159–203.

Pope, John C., ed. *Homilies of Ælfric: A Supplementary Collection*. 2 vols. Early English Text Society 259–60. London, 1967–68.

Potter, Simeon. "On the Relation of the Old English Bede to Wærferth's Gregory and to Alfred's Translations." In *Mémoires de la Société Royale des Sciences de Bohême, Classe des Lettres* 1930. Prague 1931, pp. 1–76.

Raith, Josef. *Untersuchungen zum englischen Aspekt*. Studien und Texte zur englischen Philologie 1. Munich, 1951.

Reszkiewicz, Alfred. "Split Constructions in Old English." In *Studies in Language and Literature in Honour of Margaret Schlauch*, ed. Mieczysław Brahmer, Stanisław Helsztyński, and Julian Krzyżanowski. Warsaw, 1966, pp. 313–26.

Rissanen, Matti. *The Uses of "One" in Old and Early Middle English*. Mémoires de la Société Néophilologique de Helsinki 31. Helsinki, 1967.

Robinson, Fred. C. "Syntactical Glosses in Latin Manuscripts of Anglo-Saxon Provenance." *Speculum* 48 (1973), 443–75.

Schaubert, Else von. *Vorkommen, gebietsmässige Verbreitung, und Herkunft altenglischer absoluter Partizipialkonstruktionen in Nominativ und Akkusativ.* Paderborn, 1954.

Scheler, Manfred. *Altenglische Lehnsyntax.* Berlin, 1961.

Scragg, D. G. *A History of English Spelling.* Manchester, 1974.

Shearin, Hubert G. *The Expression of Purpose in Old English Prose.* Yale Studies in English 18. New York, 1903.

Shipley, George. *The Genitive Case in Anglo-Saxon Poetry.* Baltimore, 1903.

Sievers, Eduard. See Brunner.

Sisam, Kenneth. "An Old English Translation of a Letter from Wynfrith to Eadburga (A.D. 716-7) in Cotton Ms. Otho C.i." *Modern Language Review* 18 (1923), 253-72. Repr., with "Addendum: The Verses Prefixed to Gregory's *Dialogues*," in *Studies in the History of Old English Literature.* 1953. Repr., with corrections, Oxford, 1967, pp. 199-231.

Sprockel, Cornelis. *The Language of the Parker Chronicle.* 2 vols. The Hague, 1965-73.

Stewart, Ann H. "The Old English 'Passive' Infinitive." *Journal of English Linguistics* 7 (1973), 57-68.

Stoelke, Hans. *Die Inkongruenz zwischen Subjekt und Prädikat im Englischen und in den verwandten Sprachen.* Anglistische Forschungen 49. Heidelberg, 1916.

Strang, Barbara M. H. *A History of English.* London, 1970.

Szarmach, Paul E. "Vercelli Homily XX." *Mediaeval Studies* 35 (1973), 1-26.

Tilley, Morris P. *Zur Syntax Wærferths.* Leipzig, 1903.

Timmer, Benno J. "The Place of the Attributive Noun-Genitive in Anglo-Saxon, with Special Reference to Gregory's *Dialogues*." *English Studies* 21 (1939), 49-72.

———. *Studies in Bishop Wærferth's Translation of the "Dialogues" of Gregory the Great.* Wageningen, 1934.

Toller, Thomas Northcote. *An Anglo-Saxon Dictionary, Based on the Manuscript Collections of the Late Joseph Bosworth* (1882-98) and *Supplement* (1908-21), with *Revised and Enlarged Addenda and Corrigenda* by Alistair Campbell. Oxford, 1972. [Bosworth-Toller-Campbell]

Traugott, Elizabeth C. *A History of English Syntax.* New York, 1972.

Visser, Frederic T. *An Historical Syntax of the English Language.* 3 vols. in 4. Leiden, 1963–73.

Vleeskruyer, Rudolf, ed. *The Life of St. Chad: An Old English Homily.* Amsterdam, 1953.

Wattie, J. M. "Tense." *Essays and Studies* 16 (1930), 121–43.

Wende, Fritz. *Über die nachgestellten Präpositionen im Angelsächsischen.* Untersuchungen und Texte aus der deutschen und englischen Philologie 70. Berlin, 1915.

Whitelock, Dorothy. "The Prose of Alfred's Reign." In *Continuations and Beginnings,* ed. Eric G. Stanley. London, 1966, pp. 67–103.

———. ed. *Sweet's Anglo-Saxon Reader.* 1967. Repr., with corrections, Oxford, 1970.

Whitney, William D. *The Life and Growth of Language.* New York, 1899.

Wrenn, C. L. *The English Language.* 1949. Repr., with minor revisions, London, 1960.

Wülfing, Johann Ernst. *Die Syntax in den Werken Alfreds des Grossen.* 2 vols. Bonn, 1894–1901.

Wyld, Henry C. *A History of Modern Colloquial English.* London, 1920.

Yerkes, David. "The Differences of Inflexion between the Two Versions of the Old English Translation of Gregory's *Dialogues.*" *Neuphilologische Mitteilungen,* in press.

———. "An Elementary Way to Illuminate Detail of Textual History." *Manuscripta* 21 (1977), 38–41.

———. "The Medieval Provenance of Corpus Christi College, Cambridge MS 322." *Transactions of the Cambridge Bibliographical Society* 7 (1978), 245–47.

———. "A Neglected Transcript of the Cotton Manuscript of Wærferth's Old English Translation of Gregory's *Dialogues.*" *Neuphilologische Mitteilungen* 79 (1978), 21–22.

———. "A New Collation of MS. Hatton 76, Part 'A'." *Anglia* 94 (1976), 163–65.

————. "A New Collation of the Cambridge Manuscript of the Old English Translation of Gregory's *Dialogues*." *Mediaevalia* 3 (1977), 165–72.

————. "The Text of the Canterbury Fragment of Wærferth's Translation of Gregory's *Dialogues* and Its Relation to the Other Manuscripts." *Anglo-Saxon England* 6 (1977), 121–35.

————. *The Two Versions of Wærferth's Translation of Gregory's "Dialogues": An Old English Thesaurus*. Toronto Old English Series 4. Toronto, 1979.

Syntax and Style in Old English compares the two versions of Wærferth's translation of Gregory's *Dialogues*. Old English scribes routinely respelled their exemplars, occasionally substituted one word for another, but seldom recast syntax. The translation of Gregory's *Dialogues* presents a striking exception to this practice, however. Professor Yerkes offers a rare chance to see how the language developed in grammar and style over a century or two, by comparing these two versions of an Old English text.

Bishop Wærferth of Worcester translated Gregory's *Dialogues* into English sometime between 870 and the early 890s. The anonymous scribe who revised the translation between 950 and 1050 not only changed the spelling but systematically altered vocabulary and syntax. The two versions, separated by only 60 to 175 years, differ far more than today's prose differs from that of Emerson or Arnold. Professor Yerkes analyzes four categories of revisions: in parts of speech; in repetitions of phrase or clause elements; in word order, and in the use of phrases and clauses. His study provides a valuable resource for all scholars interested in Anglo-Saxon, the history of the English language, and linguistics.

David Yerkes is Assistant Professor of English at Columbia University. His publications include *An Old English Thesaurus* (1979) and articles on Wærferth's translation in *Speculum* and in *Anglo-Saxon England*.

ᴍ ʀ ᴛ s

medieval & renaissance texts & studies
is the publishing program of the
Center for Medieval and Early Renaissance Studies
at the State University of New York at Binghamton.

mʀᴛs aims to provide the highest quality scholarship
in attractive and durable format at modest cost.